# KEN

# HOUTS

# MAXIMIZE

# YOUR

# INFLUENCE

How to *Use* the POWER
of Who *You* Are

## Destiny Image® Publishers, Inc.

P.O. Box 310
Shippensburg, PA 17257-0310

*"Speaking to the Purposes of God for This Generation
and for the Generations to Come"*

ISBN 0-7684-2301-5

For Worldwide Distribution
Printed in the U.S.A.

This book and all other Destiny Image, Revival Press, MercyPlace,
Fresh Bread, Destiny Image Fiction, and Treasure House books are available
at Christian bookstores and distributors worldwide.

1 2 3 4 5 6 7 8 / 09 08 07 06 05

For a U.S. bookstore nearest you, call
**1-800-722-6774.**

For more information on foreign distributors, call
**717-532-3040.**

Or reach us on the Internet:
**www.destinyimage.com**

# DEDICATION

To Cheryl,
who sees the King in me.


To Andrew and Julie,
whose sacrifice sustained me.


To Kerry and Joanna and Beth,
who supported me through the process.

# ACKNOWLEDGMENTS

There are special people whose lives have made this book possible because they have walked the breakthrough journey with me.

I want to thank Darrell and Mary Massier for being the God-multiplier models. Your love and friendship has sustained me. Whenever I need a story to demonstrate the vision, I always tell a Darrell story.

I thank Scott and Cathy Jones for all of their love and support of the vision. Their dedication and sacrifice encouraged me when I needed their courage.

I thank all of the pastors, coordinators, and team leaders around the world who caught the vision of the Care Ministry and have taught me as they walked the breakthrough journey with me.

Thank you to two very special Care Ministry Coordinators, our National Coordinators, Kristin Skebo and Cheryl Sandros, who have impacted my life more than either will ever know.

# TABLE OF CONTENTS

# PREFACE

The last chapter of this book, "Your Father Wants You in His Business," is the genesis of this book. The Lord gave me the vision of that only-significant-moment-of-life, standing before the Judgment Seat of Christ, and it has motivated me each day. My prayer is that you will recognize that as the only significant moment in your life and be transformed by it like I have. My prayer is that the revelation in this book will prepare you to look into the burning eyes of King Jesus with confidence and joy instead of fear and uncertainty.

I'm not referring to the fear of losing your salvation, but rather, the fear and uncertainty that you lived your life and it caused little pleasure to your King...the fear that you were created for something greater and you missed the greatness within...the fear that your life was marginalized by the deceptive culture and not maximized by a vision of the King. I'm talking about the fear of standing before Him with the eternal knowledge that you disappointed your King because you did not become the vision God the Father has of you, the fear that you disappointed your King because you did not see the God-moments of life.

*Maximize Your Influence* explains the vision that Creator-God intended for you when He created you in eternity past. This vision of you was captured and hidden by the evil one in the darkness of his kingdom. It is the vision of the restoration of all things in the Kingdom of Heaven in the new creation. It is a vision that places the Church in the center of God's eternal purpose of man instead of having the church in the back waters of being a successful business.

I invite you to join me on the breakthrough journey that will bring you to that moment before King Jesus with confidence, joy, and expectancy of eternity.

# INTRODUCTION

A new season in my life began the week I fasted, seeking out God. That week He revealed to me the Kingdom-church. I saw why the heart attitude of the King could not be contained nor defined in the maintenance culture. The church cannot follow the King because the church does not have the heart of the King. That revelation changed the direction and purpose of my life because I chose to follow the King to a higher level. To gain His heart I had to face those barriers that I had allowed to keep me in my maintenance culture, and I had to break through them. I realized that I had allowed the maintenance culture to confine the King's heart within and to marginalize my life.

In order to "maximize your influence," you must reveal the heart of the King, which is required for you to fulfill your destiny. That is how you discover the passion needed to overcome barriers within to become like King Jesus.

# 1

# THIS IS YOUR TIME!

I looked out the hotel window to see what kind of day it was going to be, and I was greeted by a brilliant morning sun. It appeared as if diamonds were scattered on the ground as the bright sunlight reflected off the frost on the grass. The sunlight felt warm and comforting on my face on this Sunday morning in December. During the short, dark days of winter, the warmth of the sun is always encouraging, and the brightness of the morning filled me with expectancy of a "God day."

As I prepared for ministering that Sunday morning, I did not know that my life was about to change. On occasion the Lord gives foreknowledge of these defining God-moments; however, this day He did not. As far as I knew, this Sunday was like a thousand other Sundays when I had ministered in churches around the world. The significant difference was that the night before, on Saturday evening, I had led the Care members in six hours of prayer, teaching them how to pray for the breakthrough anointing.

The Lord had revealed to me five powerful keys necessary for the anointing to break through, then revealed to me the Scriptures to pray for each key. That Saturday I had taught about one of the breakthrough keys, then I led the Care ministers in prayer. In about the third hour of prayer, the anointing we were praying for came upon us and elevated our prayers—and my life—to a higher level. Exercising my prayer and faith muscles created a capacity to receive more from my Father.

Often Christians struggle against satan's barriers in their lives, but they do not break through because they do not know how to pray. Christians who *should be* above and not beneath, the head and not the tail, end up coping with the adversary's oppression. I was able to train the Care members in the skill of prayer and exercising the breakthrough anointing because they made themselves available to minister to those wounded by the darkness in this world. They were not only breaking through the oppression in their own lives, but also the barriers of those they ministered to.

When we began the Care Ministries in 1987 at a local church of 4,000, we did not know that breakthrough was God's purpose. While we saw the Spirit break through in Christians' lives as they took steps of faith out of their comfort zone, and we witnessed ordinary Christians break through barriers that had held them back for years to become a miracle they never knew they could be, we did not know the Lord would have us multiply the miracle of availability tens of thousands of times.

Then the Lord called me out of 17 years of the pastorate into a trans-local ministry to multiply Care ministers in thousands of churches in scores of countries and all of these United States. We saw the same work of God: Christians made themselves available to the Spirit of God, and He broke through their fears, inexperience, and self-doubts to make them a miracle, meeting people at their point of need. It was beautiful to see—miracle after miracle because the Spirit of God broke through the enemy's oppression upon Christians.

The repeated pattern of the work of God revealed the purposes of God for giving the Care Ministry to the church. The Lord wants you, a normal Christian, to break through satan's barriers that have held you back for years so that you can become the miracle He saved you to be. He wants you to allow the miracle in you, named Jesus, to invade the lives of the hurting so they can discover His healing through you.

For years now I have seen the Spirit of the Lord break through into the lives of ordinary Christians to do extraordinary miracles, meeting the needs of the wounded, damaged, and brokenhearted. God can use ordinary Christians for divine appointments with people who desperately need God to invade their pain with His love and mercy. I have seen the joy on the face of Christians—who did not know they were a miracle—when they discover the miracle in themselves. I have seen the tears of deliverance of those who received the miracle of Jesus through ordinary Christians.

One of the greatest lies from the father of lies is that Christians are not miracles. One of the best demonstrations that Jesus is still alive in the hearts of believers occurs every Sunday in the Care Ministry. Jesus is still healing the brokenhearted, and Jesus still has mercy on those who do not deserve His love. Ordinary Christians do extraordinary exploits for God every Sunday to experience a miracle-lifestyle by making themselves available to the Lord Jesus. There are literally thousands of stories of how God works miracles through ordinary Christians.

By the anointing and grace of God, every child of God is an over-achiever. You are greater than your experiences, you are greater than your education, you are greater than your family background, and you are greater than people's perspective of you. Christ in you makes you greater. Jesus defines your limitations—nothing is impossible to him who believes! (See Matthew 17:20.) You have lots of room for growth, change, and going to a higher level. With the impossible as your ceiling, you must keep changing, keep going higher, and never be satisfied.

Teaching and modeling the Breakthrough Prayer series invited the Spirit to break through the barriers of my soul. He desired me to go to a higher level. There was a greater assignment with a greater anointing, but I had to recognize the God-moment. Expectancy is the breeding ground for miracles, and the prayer for breakthrough elevated the expectancy in my heart for God to break through.

That bright December morning as I challenged the church to live a life of vision, God was challenging me to do what I was preaching. My expectancy increased as I preached because I sensed the Lord inviting me to a higher level. He invited me to choose to follow the Spirit to breakthrough.

I heard His voice invite me at that God-moment to live my life by vision, to fulfill my destiny. That is when I declared, "This is my time! This is my year! This is my moment for breakthrough!" At that moment I drew a line in the sand, declaring to my heavenly Father, declaring to my King Jesus, and declaring to the blessed Spirit, that this was my year. I declared it also to satan and the hosts of hell that would oppose me.

This year was different. Not because circumstances had changed, not because people around me had changed—no, this year was different because I had changed. How? I had settled it in my heart. I would not back down this year. I would not be distracted this year. I would not be cast down this year. No, this was my year to break through. Whatever it took to break through, this would be the year my life would change. This year would be different because I made a determination in my heart that it was a different year. This year was different because I was declaring: "I will live by vision this year. I will keep my focus on the vision to lift me above the negative circumstances, the negative criticisms, and the contrary events. I am breaking through because I see the vision to live at a higher level."

I declared my faith for this year. It would not be the same as all of the other years thus far. This year was different. It was the year for breakthrough! There was a determination set in my spirit to stop talking the talk and, instead, to walk the walk.

In that "*charios*" God-moment, my life was changed. Circumstances did not change, yet *my life* was changed. The change was established in my heart. I had spoken it for the first time. I had determined that I would break through. A strength came into my heart where I had none before. A resoluteness rose up within.

## THE BREAKTHROUGH JOURNEY BEGAN

The breakthrough journey is not the journey of life. Everyone is on the journey of life. Everyone goes through the tribulations of life. Jesus said that in this world of darkness we will have tribulation (see John 16:33). The breakthrough journey is greater than the journey of life; the breakthrough journey will elevate your life to fulfill your destiny.

The breakthrough journey begins when you are weary of the enemy pushing you around and down. It begins when you are weary of the dark forces distracting from your destiny. It begins when you are weary of discouragement quenching the fire of the vision. The breakthrough begins when your faith determination declares: "This year the Lord will invade my life, and nothing will deter me from receiving my breakthrough."

The journey begins when you settle the issue in your heart, when you have the determination in your soul, when you declare to the Lord: "This is my time. This is my year. This is my moment." That is when the Lord sits upon His throne and takes notice of you because you are declaring what His will has been for you—He was just waiting for you to agree with Him. The Lord Jesus gets excited when you follow Him, not just in life, but to your destiny.

At that moment I began a journey—a breakthrough journey—and I invite you to join this journey with me. Break through the internal obstructions that satan has placed in your mind—those strongholds that have limited you. Break through the obstacles that the adversary has placed in your path and fulfill the vision the Lord has of you.

This is *your* time! This is *your* year! This is *your* moment for breakthrough! Join the journey toward breakthrough to live at a higher level than you have ever experienced in the Lord.

## THE MASTER OF BREAKTHROUGH

*So they came up to Baalperazim; and David smote them* [the Philistines, his enemy] *there. Then David said, God hath broken in upon mine enemies by mine hand like the breaking forth of waters: therefore they called the name of that place Baalperazim* (1 Chronicles 14:11).

*Baal-perazim* means the "master of breakthrough." The Philistine enemy came up to destroy David before he could establish his kingship. Even though David was already the anointed king, he had to destroy the enemy's dominion in Israel before he could rule as king. The Lord anointed David to empower him to accomplish the mission.

David's testimony was, "God has broken through my enemies *by my hand* like the breaking through of mighty waters." Water is a type of the Spirit of God. David knew the anointing upon his hand. When he killed the bear and the lion, he knew the anointing. When he killed Goliath, he knew the anointing. Now the anointing was upon his hand to break through the armies of the Philistines.

When I first began praying for breakthrough, there were circumstances I wanted changed, so I prayed for circumstantial breakthrough.

I prayed for months for my circumstances to change—for God to change my circumstances. When that prayer was not answered, I asked God why, and He said, "You must change so that the breakthrough will be by your hand."

What I learned through that experience was that if the Lord granted our request to be lifted to a higher level, yet we remained spiritually weak, tormented by fears, and easily discouraged, fainting at the roar of the devil, we would not be able to live at that higher level—because the higher the level, the bigger the devils. If the Lord simply delivered us from our circumstances, the adversary could easily beat us down to the level we were at before.

Many times Christians want to go to a higher level, but their faith muscle has atrophied through the lack of exercise. Their prayer muscle has not been exercised, so it is weak and ineffective. The greatest abuse of faith and prayer is not misuse, but disuse. You cannot break through with atrophied faith and prayer muscles. Weak spiritual muscles do not cause the devil to flee before you.

Only through resistance does strength come. Your faith muscles grow stronger when you apply them to the resistance from the adversary. *Adversary* means "resistor." The devil has placed resistance before you to defeat you, cause your will to weaken, to faint, and to quit. When you exercise your faith muscles, you discover that the resistance the devil uses to try to drain you, defeat you, and deflate you becomes the Lord's instrument to build a stronger faith. As you resist the adversary, strong in your faith, your prayer muscles grow stronger because the resistance exercises them to receive from the Father.

A friend of mine was ministering in Mexico. One day, while he was walking down the street with the local missionary, a group of children ran up to them begging and clamoring for money. The missionary silenced the mob of children with one word: "*Mañana*" (which means "tomorrow"). They stopped yelling, stopped jumping up and down, and looked at him, then walked away. My friend was amazed at the response of the little beggars, that they were so easily thwarted from their mission, and he asked the missionary why it worked so well. The missionary explained, "When I say no, they continue to clamor for me to give them something. But when I say 'mañana,' now I am not saying no, I am only saying 'later.'"

That is what the adversary says to you. You want more of God; you want to go to the higher level; then the enemy comes and whispers one word into your soul: "Tomorrow. Begin the journey tomorrow. Now is not the time. *Tomorrow…*"

The reason my life changed that day is that I refused to hear the deceptive word "tomorrow." "No, devil! *This* is *my* time! This *is* my *year*! This is my *moment* for breakthrough!" The journey begins when the determination is set in your soul.

This is your God-moment to look out your window to see what kind of life is before you. Your Father who loves you perfectly and completely has a brilliant life waiting for you, a life full of expectancy for the destiny He has created you to fulfill.

Settle it in your heart right now. Make this moment a God-moment by declaring out loud, "Father, I hear Your voice. You are calling me higher. I declare to You, my God, that this is my time! King Jesus, this is my moment! I will follow You fully, and whatever it takes I will follow You to my destiny in Your kingdom."

Declare to satan and all the hosts of hell: "This is my year. I will break through! You will not hold me down any longer. I will no longer listen to your deceptive word, *mañana! This* year is *my* year. *This* moment is *my* moment! *This* time I *will* break through!"

# 2

# GOD'S VISION WILL MAXIMIZE YOU!

Vision is a picture of what God is going to be and what God is going to do through me. A vision is not what *I* can *do*; a vision is a faith declaration of the big God doing something big through me this year.

> *For I know the thoughts that I think toward you, saith the Lord, thoughts of peace, and not of evil, to give you an expected end* (Jeremiah 29:11).

What makes this year different from other years? Right now, you believe that the plans the Lord has for you are not evil. The Lord has plans for peace, not of evil. If you are going to break through, you must understand that evil is not in the plans of God for you. If evil from the kingdom of darkness is in your life, that evil is satan's plan for your life, not God's plan.

God's plans are only for peace for you. *Shalom*, the Hebrew word for "peace," does not mean the absence of worry. Shalom means that the Kingdom of God invades your life. The Kingdom of God interrupts the devil's plans for your life and replaces them with shalom! Shalom means blessings, prosperity, health, goodness, and abundance. It means that the kingdom of darkness has been defeated and flees in terror from you (see James 4:7).

God has plans for you! God has a vision of your life this year to bring Heaven to earth, not only in your life, but in the lives of others. That is why Jesus taught us to pray: "Thy kingdom come, Thy will be done in earth, as it is in heaven" (Matt. 6:10).

The plan that the Lord has for us is not to deliver us out of the world, but for us to invade the "power of darkness" with the dominion of Heaven. Breakthrough is when Heaven invades the darkness on the earth. Breakthrough interrupts the devil's plans, and it intrudes upon his works with the works of God. Breakthrough is when the devil's plans of poverty, lack, sickness, division, decline, and decrease are replaced with God's plans of abundance, blessing, health, unity, increase, and growth.

God's plans are for you to reach His expected end for you, His vision of you. Vision is seeing the end from the beginning. God operates by vision, since He not only sees the end from the beginning, but He also declares the end from the beginning (see Isa. 46:10).

## GOD'S PLANS AND VISION FOR YOU

God's plans are for you to fulfill His wonderful vision for your life. When God created you, He had plans for you. The Bible says God chose you before the foundation of the world (see Eph. 1:4).

*For we are His workmanship, created in Christ Jesus unto good works, which God hath before ordained that we should walk in them* (Ephesians 2:10).

*But as it is written, Eye hath not seen, nor ear heard, neither have entered into the heart of man, the things which God hath prepared for them that love Him* (1 Corinthians 2:9).

From the foundation of the world, God the Father has had a vision of what He created you to be, and what He created you to do. God has a vision of you—a vision of His created purpose for your life, your gifts, skills, and strengths—a vision He had of you before the foundation of the world. He has plans for you to fulfill the vision He has for you. His vision will fulfill you more than any dream you have for yourself.

God's vision of you, His expected end for you, is what it is because He believes in you. He believes in you more than you believe in yourself. He believes in you because He knows what He put in you. He believes in you because He has seen the end from the beginning. No matter how satan attempts to distract you, wound you, damage you, disable you, and defeat you, your Father God has a vision of what you are going to be and do.

Don't believe the lies about you that come from the father of lies. The Father loved you so much that He sent Jesus to earth, so that you would join the journey toward your vision and enjoy the plans the Father has for you. He believes in you so much that He gave Jesus to die so you can live out the vision the Father has for you.

Believe in *God's* vision of you, not the devil's. The devil is attempting to persuade you—by pointing out your past experiences—that God's plans are evil, or that God doesn't love you, or that God doesn't believe in you. Somehow you messed up so badly that God can't fix it. His plans just can't work now because of how badly you messed up your life.

*And we know that all things work together for good to them that love God, to them who are the called according to His purpose* (Romans 8:28).

No matter how badly you messed up, no matter how much you think you ruined your life—God, your Father, has plans for you that have not changed. Do you think that the day you messed up God the Father turned to His Son and exclaimed, "What are We going to do now?" God was not surprised by your failure, and He will not be surprised when you fulfill your destiny. He has a vision of you. In fact, He is ready right now to transform your life and get you back on the breakthrough journey toward fulfilling the vision He still has of you from the foundation of the world.

This is what He wants you to know: "We know that **all things** work together for good." Maybe you're thinking, "*But you don't know how badly I messed up my life.*" No, I don't, but so what? I *do* know that *all* things work together for good.

You may say, "But you don't know *all* the things I have done. I've really messed up." I *don't* know all the things you've done, but so what? I *do* know that the Lord has a vision of you; He has plans for you, and we know that *all* things—including all the things you have done wrong— God is able to work together for your good when you love Him and recognize the moment He calls you for His purposes.

How can He work all things together for good? The Father's vision is an eternal vision because He is an eternal Father. So when He saw you from the foundations of the world, He saw what you are going to be and do for eternity.

Since God has a vision of your eternity, He has a picture of what you are going to be and accomplish by the end of your life.

Since He has a vision of you at the end of your life, He has a vision of you at the end of this year. At the end of this year, God the Father has a picture of you, what you are going to be, how you are going to change, what you are going to do. God has a picture, a vision of you at the end of this year.

If God has a picture of you at the end of this year, He has a picture of you at the end of this month.

If God has a vision of you at the end of this month, then He has a vision of you at the end of this week. God has a picture of all that you will be and do by the end of this week; He has a great vision for you at the end of this week.

If God has a picture of you at the end of this week, then He has a picture of you, a vision, an expected end, of where you are going to be, and what you are going to do at the end of this day.

Every day when you wake up, thank God for His plans for you that day. Praise Him for the vision of you He has that day. Thank Him for the God-moments He has prepared to invade your life that day with His favor, anointing, and multiplication. Thank Him for all of His blessings and the abundance of His plans and vision for you. Then ask the Holy Spirit to fulfill the Father's vision of you today.

At the end of the day, thank God for a wonderful day of fulfilling His vision of your life. Then write down, journal, all of what the Lord did today—the people you talked to, the people you had contact with—and think about the miracles the Lord wants those people to be in your life, and the miracle you can be for them.

## THE DESTINATION OF YOUR BREAKTHROUGH JOURNEY

*I will feed them in a good pasture, and upon the high mountains of Israel shall their fold be: there shall they lie in a good fold, and in a fat pasture shall they feed upon the mountains of Israel* (Ezekiel 34:14).

God's vision of you is not down in the valley. The valley experience is where you are going to fulfill God's created vision. You want to climb out of the valleys. There are three valley experiences: (1) the valley of dry bones, where you are spiritually dry and you thirst for a fresh anointing; (2) the valley of Baca, of disappointment and despair; and (3) the valley of decision where God has brought you to confront your sin that has separated you from Him.

There is a different way to relate with the Father, and that is on the breakthrough journey to the heights of the mountains of Israel. The heights of the mountains are where you get fat, where there is rest and a fresh move of the Spirit. That is where you want to be—on the high mountains of Israel.

God's vision of you is on the heights of the mountains of Israel. He has a plan each day for you to climb higher and closer to the heights of His vision of you. His best for you is on the heights of Israel. He wants His best provision for you.

The journey is what challenges you, changes you. The journey strengthens you to become like Him. The purpose of the breakthrough journey is for you to break through all of the crust upon your soul, break through all of the resistance of satan and his hosts of hell, so you can climb to the heights. As you climb, you become closer to Him and you become like Him. The objective is to become like Him—because the more you become like Him, the higher you can go. When you stop climbing, you stop changing and becoming like Him, then you are not able to go any higher. Only becoming more and more like Jesus enables you to go higher.

When you quit the journey, you stop allowing the Spirit of God to do His work in your life. Many church members are camping on the side of the road and criticizing those who are on the journey. When you stop changing, you no longer have the salt to change others, nor do you have the desire to change others. Since you have stopped, your view of the world is static. *They* have stopped changing. *They* have stopped becoming like Him.

The constant on the journey is change. The goal of the journey is change. The purpose of the journey is change. When you are changing, you are the salt of the earth. When you stop changing, you become stagnant with no dynamic life, and you are tasteless.

## THE JOURNEY IS THE GOSPEL!

The command often referred to as the Great Commission, "Go and make disciples," is better translated, "Pursue your journey [to your destiny] and make followers" (see Matt. 28:19). As you are on your breakthrough journey, inspire others to follow you on the journey. When God called you by your name, He called you on a journey to the mountain heights. His vision of you is on the heights, and the journey, the breakthrough journey, to the top is what makes you like King Jesus. When you stop and camp out, you stop being changed to be like the King.

The breakthrough journey that King Jesus commanded us to travel is to the heights of the mountains of the Kingdom of Heaven, and as you travel up to the mountains, compel others to catch the vision of life in the heights of the Kingdom.

> *For I am not ashamed of the gospel of Christ* [the Anointed King and His anointing]*: for it is the power of God unto salvation to every one that believeth; to the Jew first, and also to the Greek. For therein is* **the righteousness of God revealed from faith to faith:** *as it is written, The just shall live by faith* (Romans 1:16-17).

The gospel of the Anointed King Jesus is not just that we are saved *from* something—hell. We are saved *to* something. The gospel of the Anointed King is that we are saved to live at one level of faith to another level of faith. The righteousness of God is from faith to faith. We begin with little faith, weak faith, just enough faith to receive salvation by grace. But our destiny, blessing, abundance, and Kingdom dominion is not received at that level of faith. We feed on the Word, confess the Word, we grow strong in faith, then our faith is tested, then we go to the next level of faith; then our faith is tested again, then we go to a higher level of faith. The gospel of the Anointed King is not just a "salvation from hell" gospel; it goes beyond that to the journey from faith to faith, strength to strength, glory to glory, until we become like King Jesus. The journey to our destiny is a journey of ever-increasing faith, a journey of receiving from the Lord by faith so we can live at a higher level of faith and ascend into the mountains of the Kingdom of Heaven.

Going to a higher level always requires increased faith. Going to a higher level will always require a spiritual battle—because the higher the level, the bigger the devil. When we stop going from faith to faith, we stop experiencing the gospel of the Anointed King; we stop becoming like Him. We were saved so that we could ascend to the heights of God's vision for us. The only way to do that is to change and become like King Jesus.

That doesn't mean that we become just the nice people who attend church meetings. Remember, it is the Anointed King Jesus who kicked in the gates of hell! You and I are to be like King Jesus, who did not allow the enemy to distract Him from His mission, and our reward will be that we are raised to a higher level.

Salvation is not a static state of freedom from the fear of hell. Salvation is a dynamic journey of change, becoming like King Jesus, going from one level of faith to a higher level of faith. The hunger for the journey is to see the Spirit of God invade our lives. There is a lifting by the power of the Spirit to a higher level. Something happens beyond our effort, beyond our work, beyond what we do. That is why you change. You change for that moment of the invasion of the Spirit, then you can testify that God invaded your life, and you can experience the Kingdom of Heaven on earth at a higher level than ever before.

I was at one level, and now I am at a higher level. The adversary had us in lack, and the Lord provided abundance. We were thirsty and a fresh anointing came upon our lives. We were weak, and we became strong. We were changed by the power of the Spirit. Grace invaded our lives as we climbed to a higher level. I became more like Jesus, and I received more to become like Him.

## ARE YOU A QUITTER, CAMPER, OR CLIMBER?

*Quitters:* These are the people who have been wounded by others or who are disillusioned with events in their lives in which they seemingly had no control. They asked God to do something, and He didn't answer the way they wanted Him to, so doubts about God, or self-doubts, oppress their thinking and suppress their lives. They don't quit believing in God; they quit believing in themselves. *They* have made the mistake; *they* have done the sin that has ruined the rest of their lives. They see themselves as losers and believe that they have made the mistake that controls their future.

So they quit—quit having the passion for life, quit believing they can change or that they can reach the heights. They quit having the fire of faith within because they do not see themselves making it to a higher level. "This is as far as I can go. Others can go on, but I cannot. Life is too hard." They no longer see the vision of what the Lord wants them to become. They no longer believe, and the passion that comes from purpose is snuffed out.

They quit believing that God believes in them or wants them to go to a higher level. They quit believing that they can go to a higher level. Passion for a higher life goes away, and they accept the devil's lies about them and their future.

*Campers:* People are campers when they are stuck in the maintenance culture, maintaining what they have, not willing to change, not wanting to change, and, *worse*, thinking they do not *need* to change.

When you think you do not need to change, you cannot change. When you cannot change, you cannot ascend to the heights of the mountains. You are a camper if you decide that you have changed enough; you have arrived at the state or station that you want, and you don't want to go any higher. That is when you start to waste the reason you were created. When you stop stretching for God's daily vision of you is when you waste that day and that moment.

One of my good friends is a camper. When I first met Chuck, he was in love with the Lord, as demonstrated by the street witnessing he did. He prayed with scores of people to receive the Lord on the streets. Fast-forward 20 years and he no longer has the passion for life.

He told me his philosophy, the philosophy of a camper: "Every Sunday the benediction is for the peace of Christ to go with us. I believe that is what life is all about. God just wants us to have peace in our lives." Then he continued to tell me what he does with his life. "My wife and I play golf at least three to five times a week. We meet at the course after work and get in nine holes."

For Chuck, peace is playing golf as much as possible. That is the picture of a camper. They have no vision for their life. They have no purpose beyond feeling good about life. They have stopped having passion for their life. They are on the side of the path watching others climb the mountain, but they don't want to climb anymore.

There's nothing wrong with playing golf three to five times a week. The distractions that satan places before us many times are not sinful. You cannot condemn these activities as immoral; in fact, many are necessary. However, at the end of the day, sometimes we are led away from the journey and never discover the vision the Lord has for us. The deceiver hides our destiny from us, and we never know what we lost by the distraction.

*Climbers:* Climbers overcome mistakes and discouragement by living a lifestyle of forgiveness. A climber is not one who does not make mistakes; a climber sins, misses the path, misses God, fails, and falls on his butt in front of the judges' table. But he has a life skill that motivates him to go on.

Just because you have failed, you have sinned, you have wasted your life, does not mean that you cannot reach your destiny. You *can* reach your destiny. You can climb to the mountains of Israel because He has prepared the way for you. Jesus has paid the price for you to climb to the mountains of Israel.

In the recent Olympics, gymnast Paul Hamm was ranked number one in the world as he competed for the gold medal in the individual all-around competition, and he was favored to win. Instead of an uneventful promenade to the podium for his gold, as in life, disaster struck at one of his best events—where Paul *intended* to perform his vault and "stick" the landing. When he exploded on his jump, he became off balance, which determined his landing. Instead of "sticking" his landing, he stumbled off the mat and onto the judges' table! At that, the sports commentator declared, "*He can't win* the gold medal now. It's impossible." Then he said, "*He will remember* that mistake for the rest of his life."

That commentator's two statements are just like the devil's lies to us. Satan's message to each one of us when we fail, when we sit on the judges' table and don't stick the landing, is: "You can't win now. You will remember this moment of failure all of your life."

The devil wants you to believe that when you make a mistake, when you fail, when you fall down, it disqualifies you from reaching the heights of God's vision for you. It is impossible for you to win. You have blown any chance of fulfilling your destiny and becoming the vision the Father created you to be. You can't now; you failed. You sinned. You...(fill in the blank). Whatever way the enemy can condemn you, he will.

What Paul Hamm did is what you must do to reach your destiny. He did not remember the mistake for the rest of his life. He did not remember by the time he sat down! He wasn't thinking about his mistake; instead he was using his faith-activated imagination to see himself complete a perfect parallel bar event, which he did, and he went on to win the gold by 25/1000 of a point!

Satan is identified as the father of lies:

*Ye are of your father the devil, and the lusts of your father ye will do. He was a murderer from the beginning, and abode not in the truth, because there is no truth in him. When he speaketh a lie, he speaketh of his own: for he is a liar, and the father of it* (John 8:44).

Jesus identifies the nature of the devil as the father of lies. There is no truth abiding in him. Therefore, when he attacks you, the only way he can is out of his nature. The devil's nature is to lie.

## THE ACCUSER OF OUR BRETHREN

Also, satan is identified as the accuser of the brethren. Night and day he stands before God and recounts and exaggerates your sin before Him.

Because he hates you, he wants to disqualify you from the inheritance of being a son or daughter of God:

> *And I heard a loud voice in heaven, saying, "Now the salvation and the power, and the kingdom of our **God** and the authority of His Christ have come, for the accuser of our brothers has been thrown down, who accuses them **day** and **night** **before** our **God*** (Revelation 12:10 ESV).

Every time the devil comes before God to accuse you of sin, the Father looks at you. However, He does not see the sin; the only thing He sees is the blood of Jesus. So the devil says, "God, do You see what he/she has done?" And the Father says, "I don't know what you are talking about Mr. devil. I don't see anything but the blood of My Son." The devil realizes that God believes in the blood more than your sin. He leaves the presence of God and descends to light upon your shoulder.

Then he reminds you of your sin, your mistakes, your failures. He reminds you how bad you are, what a horrible mistake you have made. How your sin, your failure, your mistake will control your future. Your sin has ruined your life forever. You will never be able to fulfill your vision for your life. He continues to beat you over the head with the rubber hose of condemnation until you believe more in the power of your sin than the power of the blood of Jesus Christ.

After a while, you take that rubber hose of condemnation out of the devil's hand and begin to beat yourself over the head when you say, "You know what, Mr. devil? You are right. I am horrible; I don't deserve God's best; I don't deserve success. I will regret my sin the rest of my life. I will never forget what I did wrong."

While you are beating yourself up for your sin, beating yourself up for failing, for the mistakes you have made, saying the same thing the devil has been saying to you, God declares from Heaven, "You are not guilty. You are not guilty."

Why are you not guilty? Jesus took your sin and your failure and your mistake and your bad decisions upon the cross. He took your sin, your trouble, and your torment so you can have His righteousness and His good and His peace. The good that the Son of God deserves comes to you; the bad that you deserve is placed upon Him.

---

31

How do you free yourself from the tormenting thoughts from the accuser?

*And they overcame* [conquered] *him by the blood of the Lamb, and by the word of their testimony; and they loved not their lives unto the death* (Revelation 12:11).

Good news! You can conquer the accuser! You can shut his mouth. You can stamp "void" on his plans. You can be free from the torment and weight of his accusations. How do you conquer the accuser? How do you rid yourself of his tormenting thoughts? How do you stamp "void" on his plans for your future and free yourself from your sins, mistakes, and failure?

You cannot climb the mountain to your destiny, to the heights the Lord has for you, while you are weighted down with guilt and tormented with thoughts of the past. You must conquer the accuser; *then* you can go to a higher level in your life.

You conquer him by the blood of the Lamb.

How do you conquer the accuser by the blood of the Lamb? You believe that Jesus died so you can live God's vision for your life. Jesus died for your past so you can have His future.

When Jesus Christ died on the cross, He took your sins, your mistakes, and your failures upon the cross with Him. They are His and not yours. You must believe that His sacrifice of His life by shedding His blood cleanses you from sin.

*They overcame him because of...the word of their testimony* (Revelation 12:11 ASV).

How do you conquer the tormenting thoughts about your past sins, failures, and mistakes? You testify of what the blood of Jesus has done for you. *Profession* or *confession* means to "speak the same thing." To conquer the accuser you must speak the same thing God says about you! When you listen to the tormenting thoughts of the accuser, you are speaking the same thing the devil says about you. When you beat yourself down, when you magnify your mistakes and torment yourself with your failures, you are saying the same thing as the accuser.

Stop agreeing with the devil and begin to agree with what the Word of God says about King Jesus' sacrificial death on the cross for you, what His sacrifice as the Son of God means to you.

You conquer the accuser by testifying, speaking out loud, about what the blood of Jesus has done for you. Who are you testifying to when you speak out loud?

*You testify to yourself.* You must remind yourself of the freedom you have from the past by the blood of Jesus.

*You testify to the accuser.* You tell him how the blood of Jesus shuts his mouth. The blood of Jesus nullifies his plans; the blood of Jesus takes away the guilt; and the blood of Jesus frees you from the torment of his condemnation.

*You testify to the Lord Jesus.* You declare to Him that what He did on the cross has set you free. You declare to Him that His sacrifice has freed you to live out the Father's vision for you.

Why must you speak out loud? Faith comes from hearing the Word of God (see Rom. 10:17). Therefore, the more you speak the Word, the more you hear it, and the more you will believe the truth instead of the tormenting lies from the accuser.

What do you testify? Here are Scriptures revealing what the Word of God says about what the blood of Jesus has done for you. You can memorize the confession or, better yet, memorize the Scripture:

1. We overcome satan when we testify personally to what the Word of God says the blood of Jesus does for us (see Rev. 12:11).

2. Through the blood of Jesus, I am redeemed out of the hand of the devil (see Eph. 1:7).

3. Through the blood of Jesus, all my sins are forgiven (see 1 John 1:9).

4. Through the blood of Jesus, I am continually cleansed from all sin (see 1 John 1:7).

5. Through the blood of Jesus, I am justified, made righteous, just as if I'd never sinned (see Rom. 5:9).

6. Through the blood of Jesus, I am sanctified, made holy, set apart to God (see Heb. 13:12).

7. Through the blood of Jesus, I have boldness to enter into the presence of God (see Heb. 10:19).

8. The blood of Jesus cries out continually to God in Heaven on my behalf (see Heb. 12:24).

## YOU MUST HAVE GOD'S MEMORY TO HAVE GOD'S VISION

The apostle Paul says, "This one thing I do, I forget what lies behind, and stretch for what lies ahead" (see Phil. 3:13). Paul had much to forget because he agreed to the killing of Stephen. He persecuted Christians. His sins were great and that is why he said, "This one thing I do: I forget what lies behind." If you do not forget what lies behind, you cannot stretch for what lies ahead.

*And their sins and iniquities will I remember no more* (Hebrews 10:17).

God has divine amnesia! God cannot remember your sin. He cannot remember your rebellion. He just can't remember anything you have done wrong. If His memory serves Him right, all He remembers is the sacrifice His Son paid on the cross. Nothing you have done matters; it is all cleansed from His memory.

God wants you to have His memory—divine amnesia. Your sins are just not part of what you remember about your life. Your mistakes are not part of your memory. When you remember your life, you remember what the blood of Jesus has done for you. You remember what the Lord has done for you and just can't recall what the devil has done.

## THE JOURNEY BEGINS BY DECLARING YOUR DETERMINATION

If you are ready to begin the journey, repeat this declaration for yourself:

*Father God, thank You for Your vision of me that is higher than my vision of myself. Thank You for believing in me more than I believe in myself. Thank You for all that You deposited in me. I want to become that vision—Your vision of me.*

*I don't want my vision. I don't want my life or my plans for my life. I want Your plans, Your vision, Your peace, and Your expected end—Your destiny. I ask Jesus to take control of my life anew.*

*I believe in Your vision of me more than I believe in the devil's vision of me. I believe more in how You will transform me, than I believe the picture of how the enemy has attempted to disable me.*

*Because I believe that the blood of Jesus Christ, Your Son, cleanses me from all sin and because I believe I am just-as-if-I-never-sinned, I deserve Your best, I deserve Your success, and I deserve Your abundance in my life.*

*The faith in my heart puts a resolve in my soul that this day is different.*

*This day I declare to the hosts of hell: This is my time! This is my day! This is my year! I am breaking through today.*

*I say no to my fears. I say no to the disappointments of the past. I say no to the unbelief in my mind. I declare to the devil, "You are a liar!"*

*I am a miracle! I have a future! Father God, You have a vision of me, and I am beginning the journey today to break through all of the obstacles in my way and all of the obstructions upon my soul.*

*Jesus is Lord! And His vision will be fulfilled in my life. I stop just talking the talk, and today, I walk the walk. I will walk out my faith in the life and vision You have of me. Today I am breaking through to go to a higher level. Nothing the enemy does will stop me from going to a higher level. Nothing the enemy does will stop me from my breakthrough!*

*This is MY time! THIS is MY year! This is my MOMENT! It is breakthrough time for me! Look out devil, here I come!*

| 3 |
|---|

# MAINTENANCE CULTURE
# WILL MARGINALIZE YOU

At a district assembly council meeting, a pastor of a church of 200 noticed the senior pastor of the denomination's largest church humbly kneeling at the altar praying. The pastor of the smaller church told me, "I knelt close to him because I wanted to hear how the pastor of our largest church would pray."

He continued his story by saying, "I was shocked when I heard him pray, 'Father, forgive me for leading my church into the *maintenance culture*.'" The pastor of the smaller church then told me, "Ken, when I heard *him* repent of the maintenance culture, I asked myself, 'If our best and largest church in the entire nation is in the maintenance culture, what is the condition of the rest of our churches?'"

The senior pastor of the largest church in that denomination had just attended the Pastor Leadership School[1] the day prior to the district assembly. The Lord revealed to him that his wonderful, large, growing, progressive church was a maintenance-culture church. Here was a growing church, with one of the strongest small group ministries in the nation, events drawing tens of thousands of people to the church each year with contemporary praise and worship, yet the senior pastor needed to repent from leading his church into the maintenance culture.

---

[1]See author information page at the back of this book for more information.

On another occasion, a pastor of a large church of over 2,500 people was experiencing such a strong anointing when he attended the Pastor Leadership School[2] that he knew they were entering into revival. The pastor prepared his church for our upcoming Breakthrough Conference[3] by admitting to his congregation: "I have led this church into the maintenance culture, and now I must lead us out of it." He confided to me, "Our small groups, which are the strength of our church, are insulated in the maintenance culture. We have been in the maintenance culture for the last nine years."

That was a large, successful church on a 38-acre campus with a strong anointing upon the pastor, with small groups, doing everything progressive churches can do, yet they were in the maintenance culture.

A pastor of a church of 700 who embraced the *Purpose Driven Church* (PDC) vision, who had put a large display of the four bases on a church foyer wall to communicate the vision of the church as a PDC church, attended our half-day "How to Minister to Your Visitor" seminar.[4] After hearing the description of the maintenance culture and praying the prayer of repentance out of the maintenance culture, this pastor made a beeline to me at the first break and said, "My church has been in the maintenance culture for years."

Why are wonderful pastors confessing to the Lord and to their congregations that they have missed God for years? What made these wonderful men of God not see this spiritual condition in their church? If these experienced men of God have been blinded to the true spiritual condition of the churches they lead, could you be blinded to the spiritual condition that is preventing you from fulfilling God's vision for your life?

After attending our conferences, these pastors recognized that the biggest obstacle stopping them from fulfilling God's vision of them—and the greatest barrier between you and your destiny—is the maintenance culture.

---

[2]See author information page at the back of this book for more information.
[3]See author information page at the back of this book for more information.
[4]See author information page at the back of this book for more information.

## THE DECEPTION OF THE
## MAINTENANCE CULTURE

"In whom the god of this world hath blinded the minds of them which believe not..." (2 Cor. 4:4). Although in this verse the apostle Paul was referring to those in the world who do not believe, the principle is true for all: Our minds are blinded when we do not believe. Your fears, insecurities, self-doubts, and unbelief present the forces of darkness opportunity to blind the eyes of your mind.

Our big problem is that the god of this world, the deceiver, has blinded our minds because we believe not. The word translated as "blinded" in Second Corinthians 4:4 means a fog that dims and darkens our spiritual sight. With this blindness, it is not that you cannot see at all, but that you see only indistinct forms with no clarity. Often, after hearing the revelation of the maintenance culture, people tell me, "You put into words what I have been feeling." They had seen only indistinct forms, their minds blinded by the darkness.

How could such a spiritual condition be oppressing a church for years, yet the pastor did not know it? What is the darkness that is deceiving church leaders, oppressing the Church, and prohibiting Christians from seeing God's vision for their life?

## THE MAINTENANCE CULTURE

The darkness upon the church that impairs your God-vision does not necessarily originate from the worship style or the doctrines of the denomination, or whether the church has small groups or a vision statement. The darkness upon the church is in the very culture that has overcome the American church. It is a culture that maintains.

Although maintenance is an essential task of the church, the darkness has come through an overtly imbalanced investment of time, money, and people resources to maintain the church facilities, maintain the church programs, and maintain the church members. King Jesus said, "Where your treasure is, there will your heart be also" (Matt. 6:21). The imbalanced investment reveals the treasure of the American church is maintenance. The heart of the American church is embedded in the maintenance culture.

When you become a member of a church embedded in the maintenance culture, you unwittingly conform to a vision that marginalizes you in a maintenance-culture lifestyle. The fog from the maintenance-culture church blinds the eyes of your heart from seeing God's big vision of you.

## THE MISSION OF THE KING

To determine if you are oppressed in the maintenance culture, you must first determine what your mission in life is as you follow the anointed King Jesus.

There is a distinction between purpose and mission:

- *Purpose*: something set up as an object or end to be attained.

- *Mission*: a specific task with which a person or group has been charged.

A mission is a specific task with which a person or group has been charged. *The* mission of the church is not a purpose of the church. The mission of the church is not a department of the church. The mission of the church is the task with which everyone and every department in the church has been charged by King Jesus. The first step in determining if your church is in the maintenance culture is understanding the mission of the church.

Jesus declared His mission for His Kingdom-church when He commanded us to *"Go...and make disciples of all the nations..."* (Matt. 28:19 NKJV).

When disciples are no longer being made, darkness is no longer invaded, and the Kingdom is not expanded. Jesus invaded darkness to establish an ever-expanding, counter-culture, Kingdom of Heaven on the earth (see Luke 4:43). The only culture that cannot become infected with the maintenance culture is the Kingdom-culture.

King Jesus assigned the mission for the Church: to "go and make disciples." The Church is not an institution, nor is it a building, but the Church is the people; therefore, your individual and personal mission is to go and make disciples.

King Jesus' mission was to expand the Kingdom by making disciples. Since He lives in you to fulfill His mission, then His mission of life is your mission of life. Your mission of life is to expand the Kingdom of Heaven by making disciples.

This mission is not primarily a Great Commission of the church denomination to spread the gospel around the world through missions giving. It is the mission of life of every disciple who follows King Jesus. It is not an institutional commission; it is an individual mission.

I can hear the chorus of the maintenance culture using the "gift" excuse: "But Brother Houts, God doesn't want me to lead anyone to the Lord. I'm not an evangelist. I took a spiritual gifts test!"

The problem is that those "spiritual gift tests" are based upon a faulty premise: Your past experiences define your gifting. Since 95 percent of all Christians have been paralyzed by a spirit of fear from invading the gates of darkness, the spiritual gift "tests" validate the work of the spirit of fear to excuse 95 percent of all good church members from the mission of their life. The "test" interpretation of those whose hearts are embedded in the darkness of the maintenance culture is: "Do not be about the Father's business. You do not have to follow King Jesus as He invades darkness. You hide in the church building and pray."

The reason God called you by your name before the foundation of the world was to give you a mission for life, and for you to discover Kingdom significance from that mission. Therefore, when Jesus commanded, "Go and make disciples," He delegated His life mission to everyone who follows Him. If you are a disciple of King Jesus, then you are a follower of King Jesus. If you are a follower of Jesus, then you will follow Him in His life mission to make disciples.

Do you believe that this is *the* mission statement of your church? Do you believe that the reason your church building is on the street it is on is to fulfill the mission Jesus commanded, "Go and make disciples"? Then the way to measure your **spiritual dynamic** is by the level of your fulfillment of the mission.

Your spiritual dynamic is not evaluated by your spiritual habits and disciplines of prayer, nor how often you read the Word, nor how much Bible knowledge you have, nor how enthusiastically you praise God, nor how great the fellowship might be in your group. However, these spiritual habits are crucial for the purpose of providing spiritual strength— strength to fulfill your mission of life, not to maintain your life!

The question isn't: "Is your church a good church?" Nor is it: "Is your church a progressive church?" Nor is it: "Is your church a growing church?" Nor is it: "Is your church a big church?" The question you must ask is simply: "Does my church empower me with the spiritual dynamic to fulfill the mission King Jesus died for me to fulfill? Or do I excuse myself from the mission King Jesus commanded me to obey because it is outside of my comfort zone?" If you have excused yourself from the mission Jesus died for, it could be a significant indicator that you and your church are spiritually deceived in the maintenance culture.

What quality of life does your church's ministry produce in you? Do you only have the spiritual dynamic to maintain being a church member? Or do you receive a greater vision of yourself to be transformed by the Spirit of God to be a high capacity and high performance person empowered to live life at a higher level to transform a victim of darkness into a victor over darkness?

# 4

# FIVE INDICATORS OF THE
# MAINTENANCE CULTURE

There are five indicators of the type of life produced in your church. While these indicators evaluate the church, they indicate the life dynamic of the church. Is it producing the dynamic for church members to maintain their lives, or is there a dynamic to fulfill their mission of life?

The five indicators are:

1. Maintenance-culture statistics

2. Maintenance-culture standards

3. Maintenance-culture symptoms

4. Maintenance-culture ministry results

5. Maintenance-culture values

This chapter will focus on the first three indicators. The last two, maintenance-culture ministry results and maintenance-culture values, will be addressed in later chapters.

## MAINTENANCE-CULTURE STATISTICS

Statistics showing what the church's ministry is producing indicate the quality of life the church is producing. If there is dynamic life then there will be dynamic results. The Acts Church had dynamic results because they were experiencing dynamic life—not just healthy life, but dynamic life.

"Then the word of God spread, and the number of the disciples multiplied greatly..." (Acts 6:7 NKJV). In the Acts Church, the number of disciples *multiplied greatly*. Does your church have the same spiritual dynamic to multiply disciples? The Acts Church produced a quality of life in the disciples so they experienced extraordinary exploits for Jesus Christ, and the disciples multiplied!

Or does your church have these maintenance-culture statistics?

- **An astonishing 98 percent of all church growth in the American Church is church transfer.**

    You know what church transfer is, don't you? Transfer growth is via church hoppers, "cruisamanics," and steeple-chasers. Church transfer growth is growth that is produced by church members going from church to church.

    When transfer growth accounts for an astounding 98 percent of the growth in your church, it declares that church members are not on mission of life, but are slumbering in the maintenance culture. The single most revealing statistic demonstrating that your church is spiritually oppressed in the maintenance culture is that 98 percent of the growth of your church is from people who are already churched.

    This statistic reveals that church members do not have the spiritual capacity to make new disciples; they only have the spiritual capacity to recycle old church members.

    Do you know the number of new disciples your church has made this year?

    If you, like the majority of church members, do not know, what does that say about the importance of the mission Jesus died for? If the church was about the Father's business, the entire church would know the effectiveness of the church in fulfilling its mission. Since we do not know, perhaps the mission Jesus gave us is not the mission the church is fulfilling.

*Why* do we consider ourselves faithful to the Lord Jesus and to the doctrines of the Bible when 98 percent of our growth is the result of church members changing churches and not the multiplication of disciples?

Church growth and Kingdom expansion have very little in common. Kingdom expansion is the result of disciples being multiplied. Church growth does not produce Kingdom expansion when church members change churches.

• **Only 2 percent of the growth in the American Church is salvation growth.**

In all of your busyness, and I know you are very busy, but in all of your busyness, you are fulfilling the mission King Jesus gave the Church by only 2 percent.

If any corporation today would fulfill its mission statement by only 2 percent, it would be bankrupt or out of business. I want to suggest to you that the Church is spiritually bankrupt because of the spiritual oppression in the maintenance culture.

I love the church. I was born on a weekend, and I was in church Wednesday night. I have spent more time and days in church than most people, but when the church is fulfilling the mission by only 2 percent we must come to the truth that the church is spiritually bankrupt, embedded in the maintenance culture.

In the tender mercies of God we must ask, "How can we say we are obeying the Lord when we are fulfilling King Jesus' mission statement by only 2 percent?"

*Why* do we consider ourselves in the center of the will of God, while our ministry time and efforts are fulfilling the mission statement by only 2 percent?

• **Fully 95 percent of all American church members are barren.**

Church members are doing their best to be good people. You read your Bible; you pray; you attend church as regularly as you can. You are good people, but in all of your goodness, you are barren. The miracle of King Jesus living in you has become imprisoned within. He is seldom released to love the damaged and wounded in your kingdom-realm. Few, if any, have heard the wonderful story of salvation of your life. No one has discovered the love and mercy of God because of you. You attend church your entire life, marginalized in the maintenance culture.

When disciples are no longer being made, darkness is no longer being plundered.

What quality of life is demonstrated when 9.5 out of 10 church members are so fearful that they refuse to share the love of God that has been poured out in their hearts by the Holy Spirit (see Rom. 5:5)?

Now you know why 98 percent of your church's growth is church transfer—because 9.5 church members out of 10 don't talk to the wounded about the healing love in the Kingdom of Heaven.

In fact, the only people church members talk to are members of other churches. Their testimony is no longer about King Jesus, but about their church, "My church is better than your church, so why don't you come to my church?"

What quality of life is the church producing when followers of Jesus Christ no longer have a testimony about King Jesus? It is the quality of life produced in the maintenance-culture church, spiritually oppressing church members.

Why do church members think that they have a great church when the quality of life their great church produces cannot transform them into disciple-makers?

- **Over 85 percent of the churches we interview are at a plateau or in decline.**

We ask pastors to give us the attendance pattern over a four-year period, and while there may be a year or two of growth during the four years, there are also years of decline.

The end result is that over 85 percent of churches in a four-year attendance pattern produce little if any growth.

What would economists call an industry where 85 percent of the businesses were at a plateau or in decline? They would identify that industry as a non-growth industry. Economists would advise investors to stay away from the non-growth church industry. Why are some of the best and brightest Christian men and women shunning the ministry? The maintenance culture makes it a very unattractive non-growth industry.

*Why* is the church a non-growth industry?

• **Over 90 percent of the churches we interview assimilate 1-3 percent of the annual visitor volume into active core workers, or what we might describe as disciples.**

I want to define assimilation as greater than participation. Many churches think people are in their core when they are participators in another meeting other than Sunday.

Having a membership is not the same as being a disciple. I have many pastors proudly tell me of the number of church members from last year. When I ask them about how many are active, or even still attending, they do not know.

Church membership is a symptom of the maintenance culture. Most people join a church to maintain their life, not to increase capacity, nor to fulfill their life. If your church can only produce church members, you are not expanding the Kingdom of Heaven.

Here is the sad picture these statistics paint of the maintenance-culture church:

— Church transfer accounts for 98 percent of the growth in the American Church because 98 percent of the visitors are already churched. The only people who even want to attend church are church members.

— Of those visiting church members, the church has the spiritual capacity to recycle only 1 visiting church member out of 10.

— Of the 1 out of 10 recycled church members, the maintenance-culture church only has the spiritual dynamic to make active core workers of only 2 out of 100 recycled church members. When the church members in the core do not love those who are not part of the church, the core will not increase in size or spiritual strength.

Do you see the maintenance culture oppressing the quality of life of the church members who want to follow King Jesus, but who do not see the weak, anemic demonstration of the love of God?

Do you recognize that the maintenance culture has put spiritual blinders on the eyes of 95 percent of church members so they do not see the God-moments in their circle of care or in the visitors who attend your church looking for God?

But more importantly, why?

• Why is there 95 percent barrenness?

• Why is there 98 percent church transfer?

• Why is the church fulfilling the mission by only 2 percent to 8 percent?

• Why is only 10 percent retained?

• Why is only 3 percent assimilated?

• Why are there so few growing churches?

Are you satisfied with the results of your church's ministry? Why are church members satisfied with demonstrating an anemic quality of life? Why does it not grieve us all? Why is mediocrity not only accepted, but rewarded?

*In whom the god of this world hath blinded the minds of them which believe not* (2 Corinthians 4:4).

The god of this world, satan, has blinded the minds of pastors, church leaders, and church members from seeing the quality of life produced in the church embedded in the maintenance culture.

These statistics reveal that low levels of retention and assimilation are symptoms of the big problem: the spiritual condition of the church. The maintenance culture oppresses the life of the Spirit so that church members neither have the passion nor capacity to expand the Kingdom of Heaven.

## MAINTENANCE-CULTURE STANDARDS

Every business has its standards of success. The maintenance culture has defined success for the church business, and pastors are busy attempting to be successful by attaining those standards of success. Jesus said, "I must be about My Father's business" (Luke 2:49). The question we must ask is: "Are the current standards of success fulfilling the Father's business or church business?"

The Father sent His Son to begin the Family business on earth. The reason the Lord brought you and me into His Family is to be part of the Family business. If you are in the family, then you must be about the Father's business. The Father's business is to purchase the lives of His creation with His love. Jesus ransomed, bought back, the souls of mankind to fulfill God's vision of their life by His sacrifice of love. Disciples of Jesus are the buyers in the business. We are "buying back" the lives of those in our Kingdom-realm by demonstrating the love and life of God to them.

Jesus commanded us, "Go, pursue your journey, and as you journey, make followers." The picture of following Jesus is very dynamic—you are fulfilling your destiny; you are on the breakthrough journey climbing ever higher and higher in your faith walk with the Lord. As you go on your journey to your destiny, compel those who are missing their path to follow you, and you will lead them to their destiny.

The Father's business standard of success answers one question, "How many lives have been purchased by My love?" He asks, "How much do you invest My Church's resources of money, staff time, and volunteers in the purchase of lives?" The maintenance culture asks, "How much money do we spend maintaining the church members, maintaining church facilities, and maintaining church programs? How much money have church members given the church to fulfill the maintenance mission—maintaining them?"

The standards of success for an institution or business are defined by the culture of that business. Therefore, identifying the true standards that communicate success will identify the culture of that institution. What the culture defines as success will motivate those within it to pursue those success standards.

So if your church has the maintenance-culture standards of success, then the maintenance culture is defining, motivating, and controlling the activities and time invested to become successful. Standards of success demonstrate the real mission.

What we measure demonstrates our priorities because "what gets measured, gets done."

Although the church may declare that its mission is to make disciples, the standards of success will demonstrate if the actual mission is to maintain church facilities, maintain church members, and maintain church programs.

The question isn't: "Are you a successful church, or a progressive church, or a growing church, or a big church?" Those all can be the result simply of being in the right location at the right time, without being about the Father's business.

What are the standards of success in the maintenance-culture church business?

- **Increased attendance is *the standard* of the maintenance culture.**

  So much of what the church does is governed by this one standard because increased attendance is success. Whatever draws big crowds is success. Disciples may not be made, the Kingdom of God is not expanded, but the church is successful because the attendance was good. When every meeting is judged by this standard, then the church will never reach its mission.

- **Increased income is the standard of the maintenance culture.**

The budget is a huge standard of success in the maintenance culture. Pastors will be promoted by their ability to increase cash flow. You can have a strong budget and large cash reserves, but very little of it is invested in the mission to make new disciples.

When I ask a pastor what the attendance average for the month or the year is, he can usually tell me. I ask a pastor the giving for the month and for the year, and he can tell me. I ask a pastor how many new disciples the church has made this year or month, and he says, "I'll have to check on that." What is wrong with this picture? The deception of the maintenance culture has redefined success from Kingdom expansion to the same motivation of the world system of size and money.

- **Increased Sunday school or small group attendance is the standard of the maintenance-culture church.**

The maintenance-culture church standards ask the wrong questions of commitment because the standards of the maintenance-culture church are so low. The maintenance-culture church standard of successful assimilation is getting people to attend another meeting other than the weekend services.

I was conducting a pre-Breakthrough Conference staff consultation for a church of 1,600 when one of the staff asked, "How about spiritual maturity?" I responded by asking, "What do you mean by spiritual maturity?" The staff person defined spiritual maturity as "knowledge of the Word."

I then asked this question, "Do Christians become spiritually mature by hearing the Word or by doing the Word?" Spiritual maturity does not occur in Sunday school class by hearing the Word and gaining knowledge. The apostle Paul tells us, 'Knowledge' puffs up, but love builds up" (1 Cor. 8:1 ESV). In the maintenance culture, hearing is doing. In the maintenance culture, knowledge, not application of the Word, is spiritual maturity.

James told us, "But be doers of the word, and not hearers only, deceiving yourselves" (James 1:22 NKJV). Spiritual maturity is experienced by those on the journey climbing to the heights of the mountains of Israel, compelling others to join the journey to their destiny.

The Acts Church multiplied disciples because the Church had the spiritual dynamic to produce disciples who were multipliers. The Acts Church did not produce church members, but multipliers.

The maintenance culture is a fog that keeps us from seeing the vision of the disciple, so the bar is lowered to a church member. The maintenance-culture church produces participators in church programs, not disciples of leaders.

- **Facilities are the standard of the maintenance culture.**

I consulted with a large church that had just completed a 16-million-dollar campus. It was beautiful. Knowing that I was working with the other large churches in the denomination, a man asked me if his church was the largest and best of them. I told him that it was, because it was.

However, the very question revealed that he was in the maintenance culture. If he had asked me how many disciples the other churches had made, and how they had used their facilities to multiply disciples, then he would have revealed a different standard.

When you stand before Jesus, He will not say, "Boy, I was impressed with that church complex you built."

The maintenance culture is impressed with buildings, money, and size—the same standards of the world.

- **Missions giving is the standard of success in the maintenance culture.**

We must sow into the fields that are responsive to the gospel. We must sow into missions, and we must sow into the mission of the local church. King Jesus told us we would be His witnesses to Jerusalem, Judea, Samaria, and to the uttermost parts of the earth (see Acts 1:8). Maintenance-culture churches spend their budget on maintenance-culture church issues. There is no end to what the church can think it would be good for the church to have—for themselves.

Many pastors consider the money they spend on maintenance of church members, facilities, and programs as their giving to the local church mission. Spending money on a new roof is maintenance, not mission.

Local missions investment has a direct result of either more unsaved and unchurched people having an opportunity to hear the gospel and respond to the gospel, or equipping members to become disciple makers. That is missions.

In the maintenance culture, increased attendance is success, increased giving is a success, increased Sunday school attendance is a success, and increased missions giving is a success. Those are standards of the church business in the maintenance culture.

Although all of those are good to see occur, they are not the best. They are not the standards of success in the Father's business. The maintenance culture substitutes man's good for God's best.

Do your standards reveal that you are about church business or the Father's business?

## Maintenance-Culture Symptoms

There are symptoms of church business behavior that reveal whether or not the maintenance culture is directing the course of your church—symptoms that indicate the church is deceived by the god of this world who has blinded our minds. Here are some of the symptoms.

- **At least 95 percent of pastor and staff time is invested in maintaining the church.**

The staff does not have the time to fulfill the mission because they are so busy! The staff is busy making hospital calls, visiting church members, having dinner with church members, counseling church members, producing and maintaining programs for church members, and meeting after meeting with church members.

The staff is consumed in nurturing and maintaining church members. That is what they are paid to do. The pastor and staff do not have the time to think of reaching out beyond the church to minister to anyone else.

If a pastor or staff person would invest their time in fulfilling the mission by leading a victim of darkness into the Kingdom, some of the church folks would complain because the pastor did not come by and see them. There is always a church member who will take your time in the maintenance-culture church.

If your staff meetings are about church calendars, church space, church programs, and not about engaging the departments in the Father's business, then you are in the maintenance culture.

- **The board spends 95 percent of their time and the church's money on the maintenance.**

The board will spend hours discussing what type of composition for the roof. They will spend months talking about what type of parking lot. They will have committees studying carpet. Then someone walks in and suggests, "Why don't we get somebody saved?" And the response is, "It's not in the budget. Anyway, have you seen how busy we are? We don't have time to get anyone saved." The symptom of the maintenance culture is that we are investing our time and money on things and not on people.

A friend of mine told me about his experience on a church board when they took five minutes to spend $50,000 on a new roof to make sure they didn't have problems in the future. Then the next week someone asked the same board for $2,000 for outreach and it took up the whole meeting. Why were they so quick to spend $50,000 on a roof that was not in need of immediate repair, but struggled to approve $2,000 for outreach? In the maintenance culture, spending $50,000 on a thing is easier than $2,000 on the mission.

If your leadership spends more time discussing and buying *things* instead of investing in *people and mission*, it is a behavioral symptom of the maintenance culture.

• **Members are too busy to invest their time in church.**

The number one excuse why church members are not involved in ministry is that they are too busy. Church members are not too busy. Every person invests in what they value. When it is important to them, they will make the investment of their time and money. If is not important to them, they won't. When they do not invest their time in the Father's business, it is because they do not see value in the investment. It is that simple.

When church members say they are too busy, they are saying that church does not have enough value for them to invest in it. Everyone has the same amount of time; often church members do not value the church they attend enough to invest in it. Why? The maintenance culture does not provide vision and passion to motivate anyone. Maintenance is not an exciting vision. Maintenance does not create passion.

• **Members are *unmotivated* to care for the unchurched.**

A pastor told me his experience with this maintenance-culture symptom. He reported, "I offered a class on how to lead someone to the Lord, and no one came."

The symptom of the maintenance culture is that Christians don't care about the mission. How do your members communicate their care about the mission? How many demonstrate that they do not care?

When you ask church members why they have not led anyone to the Lord, they say, "It's not my gift; I took a test." The motivation for the mission of life is not gifting; it is a vision of life that has a mission. The maintenance-culture vision of a church member is to be devoted to being the best church member one can be without being about the Father's business. You can be a church member and never make a difference in someone's life. You can be a church member and never make a disciple.

If the members of your church do not have a vision of living a life with mission, but rather give excuses why they are not responsible for the mission of making disciples, then they are in the maintenance culture.

• **Members are *unskilled* to be caregivers.**

Another behavioral symptom of the maintenance culture is unskilled church members. The maintenance-culture church does not invest in training, only in maintaining and nurturing. In the maintenance-culture church, even the few church members who want to do something, don't have the skills to impact someone for Christ. Does your church train the members in the ministry skills needed to meet people at their point of need and make disciples?

If your church members do not know how to engage someone in conversation to discover their need; if they do not know how to invite someone to pray with them about their need; if they do not know how to share their testimony; and if they do not know how to share the gospel—they are untrained. They are untrained, and that is the number one reason they don't share the gospel—they don't know what to do. No one will try to do something if they do not know what to do or how to do it. A behavioral symptom of the maintenance-culture church is untrained church members.

• **Members are *not mobilized* to make disciples.**

The maintenance-culture church does not know how to mobilize their church members to make disciples. The most frequently asked question when we conduct the Breakthrough Conference is, "Can you really get 20 percent of my congregation to volunteer for a visitation program?" My answer is, "Of course not, but I have been motivating Christians for 15 years to fulfill their destiny." The greatest need in the church is motivating the people of God to fulfill the reason they were saved. The maintenance-culture church does not motivate church members for the mission because it is not the mission of the maintenance-culture church.

- **Approximately 80 percent of the people in the congregation are *not core members.***

    Here is the biggest behavioral symptom of the maintenance culture: Eighty percent of the congregation that sits in front of the pastor during the weekend services are not core workers. They are not disciples; they are only church members. The behavior of the maintenance-culture church member is to use the church to be nurtured and maintained, but not to invest in it.

So as you are successful in the maintenance culture by increasing in attendance, you create a problem of more and more attenders and proportionately fewer active core workers to serve all the attenders. Growing churches in the maintenance culture create their own problem because they can only make church members and not disciples.

# 5

# THE MAINTENANCE CULTURE'S
# IMPACT UPON CHURCH GROWTH

After 15 years of interviewing thousands of pastors to provide them with a free ministry analysis[5], we have discovered the factors that determine the pace and effectiveness of the growth of your church. The easiest way to see the impact of the maintenance culture upon your church is by evaluating the results of your church's ministry toward those who are not members of your church.

## ANNUAL VISITOR ATTENDANCE VOLUME

For example, you can tell that the maintenance culture is impacting your church when: *The annual visitor attendance volume equals the total weekend attendance.*

The *annual* visitor attendance volume is what you must evaluate, not your weekly visitor attendance, because you miss the big picture and the growth potential when you only view it weekly. Your annual visitor attendance volume includes not only your weekly visitor attendance, but special events such as Easter Pageants, Christmas programs, Friend Day, Independence Day Celebrations, Mother's Day, VBS, and Super Bowl Sunday. Every event or special Sunday that

---

[5]See author information page at the back of this book for more information on how to receive your church's ministry analysis.

would generate visitors attending your church would be included because with the Care Ministry you will have 20 percent of your congregation engaged in ministering to them.

Many churches leave growth opportunities on the table because they have no way of ministering to all of the visitors who walk onto their campus. With the Care Ministry you will; that is why our analysis includes every visitor from all of your events because each one can become a disciple through personal ministry.

If your church has 200 people attending Sunday morning, the national average visitor attendance is to generate 200 visitors in a year. If your church has 7,000 total attendance on the weekend, you will generate 7,000 visitors in a year.

When the annual visitor volume of your church equals the number of people attending your church on Sunday, it is an indication of the maintenance culture. While many pastors consider that a lot of people because they never considered the annual visitor volume, it represents less than one visitor per year per attender in your church.

That is true for Baptist, Methodist, Nazarene, Lutheran, Pentecostal, evangelical, progressive, contemporary, and PDC churches. It's true in California, Texas, Florida, New York, Minnesota, Kansas, and Ohio, every state and every Canadian Province.

## FOUR FACTORS FOR GROWTH

There are four factors of church growth:

1. The number of visitors you generate

2. The number of visitors you lead

3. The number of members intentionally invading their kingdom-realm

4. The number of disciple-makers you generate (which will be discussed in the next chapter)

For 15 years my team and I have interviewed thousands of pastors, including some of the fastest-growing churches in America, as well as some churches that haven't grown in 50 years. As I interviewed them, I was comparing their experiences with a book that stated 15 reasons why churches grow.

One of the reasons given for why churches grow was adequate parking. If you don't have that, your church won't grow. Another factor for growth was that you had to have more than 80 percent capacity in your sanctuary. Another one was that you had to have nice women's restrooms.

I would interview the pastors experiencing dramatic growth and ask them about their parking, and they would tell me, "Ken, we have people parking on the street."

I would ask them about their seating capacity, and they would report, "We are putting chairs in the aisle." Then I would ask them about their women's restroom. The pastor would answer, "I don't know. I haven't been in there lately."

Then I would interview the pastor of a plateau church about his parking, and he would tell me, "We repaved it last year and we have plenty of parking." Then I would ask him about his seating capacity, and he would tell me, "We have plenty of seating available." I would ask him about his women's restroom, and he would say they just remodeled it.

The dynamics that *produce* growth of the local church are not seating capacity, nor parking spaces, nor nice restrooms, nor carpet. So what does produce growth?

## 1. The number of visitors you generate

My research of 15 years has discovered only one common factor to all the fastest-growing churches in America. They all have four to five times the national average of annual visitor volume.

Your visitors are your future church; therefore, the number of visitors you generate is one of the most important dynamics that will determine how large a church you will pastor in the future.

Generating visitors is what fast-growing churches do. Churches that are not growing do not generate a greater annual visitor attendance volume. If your church has the national average of visitors, then you must begin discovering how to generate more visitors, and specifically how to motivate your members to bring their friends to church.

The key to generating visitors is not to market to Christians to attend your church. The key is to produce events that the unsaved will want to attend. (Gospel song night is not going to bring unsaved people to your church. That is a maintenance activity to entertain your church members.)

A Super Bowl party for the men of your church to invite their friends to have fun at church is an outreach event. One pastor responded, "I can't have beer commercials in my church!" I recommended that during the commercials he could have power-point presentations about the church and upcoming events that the audience of men would be interested in. During half-time he could have a testimony from an athlete to give men an opportunity to receive the Lord.

## 2. The number of visitors you lead

The greatest dynamic determining size and effectiveness of your future church is how you engage your members in leading your visitors into the community of the church. Visitors are your future church. The only way they will become part of your core is for a trained member who is in the core to love them and lead them into the core of your church. The reason the maintenance-culture church does not grow is that the members do not invest their time in the future church, the visitor, but only in the current members and programs.

This Sunday's attendance and offering are the results of past ministry, so when you measure today's attendance and today's offering, you are measuring the results of your past ministry. Most churches do not have the evaluation instruments to measure the effectiveness of their current ministry nor what type of impact it will have upon their future church. Therefore, most churches are reactive, not proactive, because they only know how to measure the results of their past ministry.

If you do not know the factors that determine the growth of your future church, you cannot measure how well you are meeting the needs of your future church. When you are not measuring how well you are meeting the future church's needs, you will not be able to meet the needs when they want you to meet their needs. You will be behind the ministry opportunity. You are not just unaware of their needs, but you are incapable of meeting their needs. People quickly recognize that their needs are unimportant and leave to find a church that values them and their needs. Often, growing churches that neither measure nor profile their visitors are ill-prepared to lead them because they do not have the ministry nor programs for their future church.

What determines your future church? The two groups that comprise your future church are the visitors and your Kingdom-church. The Kingdom-church is comprised of the relationships your members have with the unsaved and unchurched. Since over three-quarters of your visitors are invited to attend by your members, the whole process of multiplying disciples originates with engaging your members in the mission.

## UNDERSTANDING YOUR FUTURE CHURCH

Visitors are your future church. What must you measure to proactively understand what your future church looks like? You must measure your visitor attendance, visitor profile, visitor retention, and visitor bonding.

### Visitor Attendance

Visitor attendance is determined by your church's "invite-ability dynamic." Between 75 percent and 96 percent of your visitors attend because someone in your church invited them. When you measure visitor attendance you can not only project your future church attendance, but also evaluate how excited your members are about inviting their friends to their church.

What is a church invite-ability dynamic? Every church has a dynamic that motivates its members to invite their friends to church, or motivates people to attend church without their friends. I ministered in a church of 1,800 in Amarillo, Texas. A man recruited to lead a Care Ministry team approached me to tell me how the Care Ministry had changed his attitude about his church.

He said, "Ken, I have been a member of this church for 12 years, but I have never invited a friend to my church. But now with the Care

Ministry, I want to invite my friends." Astonished at this admission, I asked him why he had not invited any of his friends, and how the Care Ministry had made a difference. He informed me, "I was afraid that my friends would not be accepted and cared for, so I did not invite them."

Church members will not take the risk of offending their friends by bringing them to a church that will not care for them, nor make them feel important. The "invite-ability" dynamic is not your carpet; it's not your building—it's your culture.

The maintenance-culture church is a group of church members ignoring visitors because they are focused only on themselves. The maintenance culture determines the growth of your church in two ways: First, visitors perceive the maintenance culture and sense this church does not consider them important. Second, with even more impact on your future church, your members perceive the maintenance culture and will not be motivated to invite their friends to church.

I am sure your church graphs your weekend attendance. I would encourage you to graph your visitor attendance because it will give you a picture of what the attendance of your future church will become.

### Visitor Profile

Not only do you need to measure your visitor attendance, you must profile your visitors. I asked a Care Ministry church pastor how the ministry had impacted his church of 1,000. He told me, "It has reshaped our ministry because prior to the Care Ministry we did not know the needs of our visitors. When I began to meet with them, minister to them, I discovered that you were wrong, Ken."

I asked Pastor Greg, "How was I wrong?"

He responded, "You said visitors come to church with needs, but in our church, 75 percent of our visitors attend church not just in need, but in crisis."

The pastor continued, "When we began to discover what their needs were, we realized that the material we were receiving from headquarters was not targeting our future church, but our past church. We had to get new material and organize new classes to meet the needs of our future church." Then he said, "I am happy to report that this church is assimilating, not just retaining, but assimilating 33 percent of the visitors with the Care Ministry."

When profiling visitors, consider aspects such as: Are they single, in a blended family, married, or single with children?

In many major metropolitan areas, over 50 percent of the population is single. In one church I consulted with, at least 67 percent of their visitors were single. They did not have a single's ministry so they were unprepared for 67 percent of their visitor harvest. They were glad I helped them see their harvest.

- Do we have ministries for their specific situation?

- Do they know anyone in the church?

- Are they churched, unchurched, de-churched, saved, or unsaved?

- What are their heart-felt needs?

- What motivated them to attend our church?

- What are their perceived needs?

### Visitor Retention

You must measure and evaluate if the ministry your church provides to the visitors, your future church, is as effective as it is to your current church. Do you know the needs of your visitors, and are you meeting them at their point of need? Do you have members trained to relationally connect with them the first Sunday they attend? How are you evaluating the effectiveness of your visitor retention?

### Visitor Bonding

This is the most important factor to measure because retention does not produce disciples, only attenders. A disciple is a follower who will invest his or her time and money in the church. The maintenance-culture church invests its resources, not in bonding a visitor to become a disciple, but in retaining, because attendance is the standard of success. Once you change your goal from church member to disciple, then you will invest your resources into that which makes disciples.

What is your structured process to communicate the love of God to bond the visitor to your church? What are the steps needed to make a disciple? The lack you are experiencing due to the maintenance culture will be filled by making disciples of your future church.

Most churches have the capability to bond between 1 percent and 3 percent of their *total annual visitor volume*, which should be the measurement, not the number in your membership class. The majority of people who attend a membership class have determined to become members. Although the distance between bases is great, you must build a bridge between church attendance and first base. (The baseball diamond analogy comes from Rick Warren's *Purpose-Driven Church*. First base signifies church membership.) That bridge is a personal relationship bonding them to the church.

Who is recruited and trained to love people into the church? How many members are relationally bonding visitors into your church? If you don't have members relationally bonding visitors into your church, you are not going to produce disciples, because the only way disciples are made is by the love of God through relationships.

Tasks do not make disciples of Jesus Christ. Have you heard the term "plugged in"? As in, "We've got to get them 'plugged in'"? People are not electrical appliances to be plugged into your institutional organization. They are people who will be bonded by love to the Body of Christ (see Col. 2:19).

The Body of Christ is not made up of tasks or job descriptions. The Body of Christ is created by loving relationships bonding people together to fulfill their mission and vision for their life.

So the question is: How many members in your church are trained to relationally assimilate visitors into your church?

# 6

# MAINTENANCE-CULTURE VALUES

## WHAT IS A VALUE?

A value is the conviction of the way things should be. Values are the rallying point for the ideal conduct for which we strive. Church members express it when they say, "That's just the way things are done around here." Values are the principles upon which the church will be built and the vision of the church and the church member. Values are the core motivator for church members.

There are two types of values:

1. Maintenance-culture values

2. Kingdom-culture values

Maintenance-culture values produce church members. Kingdom-culture values produce disciple-makers. Therefore, if your church has the maintenance-culture behavioral symptoms, it is because it has the maintenance-culture values. If your church has the maintenance-culture statistics, it is because it has the maintenance-culture values. If your church has the maintenance-culture standards of success, it is because it has the maintenance-culture values. If your church's ministry results are low retention and ineffective relational bonding, it is because of the maintenance-culture values, not because of the wrong programs.

I was teaching a church leadership team about the maintenance culture, and one of the board members objected to the idea that their progressive church with contemporary music could possibly be spiritually oppressed by the maintenance culture.

To prove to me that his church was free of the spiritual oppression from the maintenance culture, he proudly informed me that their evangelism committee discussed evangelism at least 50 percent of the time! His "proof" revealed how much the church was deceived by the darkness in the maintenance culture in several distinct ways.

First, because the maintenance-culture values deny *the* Mission that King Jesus died for. To "go and make disciples" is *the* Mission of the *church*. The maintenance-culture values regulate it as only *one* of several missions of the church. When *the* Mission becomes just a mission, then few, if any, disciples are made.

When the Mission becomes a mission, this "mission" of the church receives the least money in the budget, the least time on the calendar, and the fewest members get involved. When *the* Mission becomes *a* mission, then it just seems like we never get around to "going and making disciples." The excuse is, "You just don't know how busy our church is."

Second, having an "evangelism committee" compartmentalizes the mission, sanitizing the other church members from being engaged in the Mission, and justifying their Mission disengagement. After all, they can easily say, "I am not part of that committee." So the vast majority of church members miss their mission of life because it is a department, not the Mission.

Third, the only people in the church who talked about the Mission spent only 50 percent of their already limited committee time discussing the Mission they had been given.

Finally, the final evidence that his "proof" exposed the maintenance-culture values was that the end result of the committee was not disciples, but just talk.

Why did that church leader think his wonderful, progressive church did not have the maintenance-culture values? I am sure he could believe it about other churches in town. The ones that were not quite as progressive, the ones that still had a traditional worship style—those had to be the maintenance-culture churches. However, the maintenance culture is not defined by current hot button church issues, but by biblical standards.

The problem with deception is that we do not know we have the problem. It is always the church down the road, or it is the other denomination that is wrong. It is much easier to see the error in others. It is much easier to identify the maintenance culture in other churches than to see it in our own church, and still much harder to see in our own lives.

Here is the problem many church leaders do not see. The pastor sets forth biblical values for his church. He thinks that because he has taught them and they are in the bulletin and taught in the church membership class, that they are the values of the church. *Taught* values are not necessarily *embraced* values.

How can you know if the values you teach are the values embraced by your church members? An embraced value determines the behavior of the church and church member. If the taught values are only known by a few, and the taught values are motivating and changing even fewer, then they are not the values of the church.

Often, taught biblical values are not the embraced values; instead, the maintenance-culture values are the embraced values of the church. The pastor is frustrated with the attitude and behavior of his church members because their behavior is not the same as the values he has set forth. The maintenance-culture values are motivating the church, not his taught values. It is not what values people are taught, but what values *motivate* them that are the embraced values, and those will determine the course of your church.

The question to ask is: What percentage of my church is motivated by the maintenance-culture values?

## FOUR VALUE DYNAMICS IN THE HEARTS OF CHURCH MEMBERS

Often church leaders do not understand the power of values in the church, and the result of good church members missing their mission of life. They see their church members resistant to change. They see their church members disengaged with the mission. They see the church members disinterested beyond their own needs, and they do not know why.

It is because there are four dynamics that values have in the hearts and minds of church members. Once we understand those dynamics, then we will understand why church members have the behavior they have.

### 1. Values define the vision of the church and church members.

A vision is a picture of what we are going to be and do. The vision of what a Christian is going to be and do is defined by the values. The picture of what the church is to be and do is defined by the values. Although churches may have a vision statement, if the church members are not following the vision, it is because their values are defining their life, not your vision statement.

If you want to know what vision your church members have of being a Christian is, look at their behavior. If they are maintaining their Christian life and maintaining church facilities, church programs, and church members, then their vision is defined by the maintenance-culture values. If they are disengaged from the Mission, if 95 percent of your members are barren, it is because their vision of a Christian is defined by the maintenance-culture values.

### 2. Values drive the motivation of the members.

The reason so many church members sit in the pews doing nothing is that they are motivated to sit and do nothing. All behavior begins with motivation. Positive motivation produces positive behavior; negative motivation produces negative behavior. There is a reason why people do what they do.

Values are the motivation for the action and behavior of church members. Kingdom-culture values motivate people to a behavior to stretch to a higher level to make disciples. Maintenance-culture-driven values motivate people to a behavior to sit and do nothing, to maintain what they have.

### 3. Values direct the course of the church.

The behavior and motivation of church members will direct the course of the church. Where the church is going, or not going, is determined by values. The church calendar reflects the values of the church. If it is full of events to maintain and entertain church members, it is because the maintenance-culture values are directing the course of your church.

If there are few events on the church calendar attracting the unchurched and unsaved for the purpose of proclaiming the Good News to make disciples, that behavior reveals that the course of the church is directed by the maintenance-culture values.

### 4. Values determine the culture of the church.

Since the culture of the church is determined by the behavior of the church members, and the behavior of the church members is motivated by the values, therefore, the values determine the culture of the church.

## KINGDOM-CULTURE VALUES VERSUS MAINTENANCE-CULTURE VALUES

Kingdom-culture values provide the Christian life with vision and mission. It is not about the values of an institution, nor about having a "church home." Values express the quality of life pursued by those within the church. Values express the mission and vision that motivate Christians to join the journey to the mountain heights of Israel. When a church has inspiring values, people will rise to live at the level of those values.

In the maintenance culture, the values are for the purpose of maintaining the people within that church. In a Kingdom-church, the values motivate people to live at a higher level, to live a life of vision and mission.

Here is a value comparison between maintenance culture and Kingdom culture:

| Kingdom-Culture Values | Maintenance-Culture Values |
|---|---|
| God is a big God. | God is disengaged. |
| Empowered Ministry | Nice People |

| | |
|---|---|
| Availability | Attendance |
| Needs-meeting | Self-focused |
| Disciple-maker | Student |
| Kingdom-Church | Building Church |
| Relationships | Meetings |
| Team Ministry | Things Committees |
| Training | Nurture |
| Empowering Leadership | Teacher-Caregiver |

### Maintenance-Culture Value: A Disengaged God

In the maintenance culture, God is disengaged because you don't need God to maintain your life; you only need God when you are in trouble. God is disengaged in the maintenance-culture church because you don't need God to work miracles when you are maintaining. You can maintain your church programs, members, and facilities on your own ability. The church can function just fine without God. It is the value of self-reliance, and not dependency and faith in the Lord.

How do you know when God is disengaged? When no one has a story of the Lord invading their lives. Few, if any, are receiving the Lord, and even fewer of them are actually disciples engaged in the ministry and mission of the church. The church members seem to be using God to maintain their Christian life, rather than serving the Lord with all of their heart. It is difficult to have passion in praise when God is disengaged.

### Kingdom-Culture Value: God Is a Big God

The values of the Church must begin with the value of God—what type of God do we serve, follow, and celebrate?

I learned this value from the pastor of the world's second largest church in Argentina. His church grew from 0 to 500 the first year, then 500 to 5,000, then 5,000 to 50,000, then 50,000 to 150,000, then 150,000 to 250,000 in less than 10 years! He had a big church because He had a big God!

He told me: "Ken, think big! For as big as you think, God will do it. Plan long-term. For as long-term as you plan, God will accomplish it!"

God is a big God, and that big God dwells in you. His name is Jesus! Do you believe Jesus wants to do something big in your city? Do you believe Jesus wants to do something big in your church? Do you believe Jesus wants to do something big through you? The big God is doing something big in your city, and big in your church begins with the big God doing something big through you.

In the Kingdom-church we celebrate a big God that is big in me! A value is "this is the way things are done around here." The way things are done in the Kingdom-church is that "God does big things around here!" In the Kingdom-church we pray for God to break through into our lives.

Our praise has passion when we believe in a big God who invades our lives. Our prayers intensify and increase in frequency when we believe God hears our prayers. Our lives have mission when we serve a big God.

Is your God disengaged because you can maintain your church life without Him, or do you have a big God doing big miracles in your life? What is your value?

### Maintenance-Culture Value: Nice People

In the maintenance culture we want the people who attend our church to be nicer than the people who don't go to church. You can't come here unless you are nice—"just like us" is the attitude in the maintenance-culture church.

In the maintenance-culture church our testimony is not about how Jesus has transformed our lives; rather, our testimony is that we are nice. "People will know I am a Christian because I am nice." We are nicer than the people who do not go to church. The problem with that is there are people who don't go to church who are nicer than some people who do.

There has to be something more dynamic than nice to demonstrate the big God who lives in me.

Our theology declares that the God who created Heaven and earth lives in me; the Jesus who was raised from the dead lives in me; the Christ who defeated the devil and all of his hosts of hell lives in me; but the best He can do is make me nice. God is bigger than making you nice.

### Kingdom-Culture Value: Empowered Ministry

When you have a big God, then you are empowered to do big things! You are empowered to impact the world you live in with the love and power of God, empowered to change lives, empowered to meet needs, empowered by the Spirit to show them the life, power, and love of God.

Jesus disarmed the principalities and powers. "And having spoiled principalities and powers, He made a show of them openly, triumphing over them in it" (Col. 2:15).

Jesus made a public spectacle of defeating all the forces of evil and darkness when He was raised from the dead. You are empowered with the same Jesus that triumphed over them. He lives in you so you make a public spectacle of their defeat. How do you demonstrate that the devil is defeated? By having the power of God in your life, not just to overcome sin, but to change the eternal destiny of those who are in darkness, damaged, and disabled by the devil.

You are to be just like Jesus. Jesus' life was not a defensive life that just did not sin; He took that sinless life and transformed others with it. The Jesus in you is empowering you to go beyond the nice life of a good church member. Be empowered like Jesus. Transform someone's eternal destiny because you have overcome the devil.

Jesus lives in you to do more than defend your life from sin. Jesus said, "The gates of hell shall not prevail against [you]" (Matt. 16:18). Gates don't attack. The only way the gates of hell will not prevail is when we attack the gates. How do you attack the gates of hell? By kicking in the gates of hell and plundering the strongman's house.

You are empowered by the Jesus in you not only to transform your life, but to make a public spectacle of Jesus' defeat of the devil by kicking in the gates of hell and rescuing others from darkness. That is the power you have. You are empowered for ministry because the Jesus who defeated all the host of hell lives in you.

Do you have the value of being a nice person, or are you an empowered minister?

### Maintenance-Culture Value: Attendance

This one value governs much of what the church is about. The problem is, there may be a big crowd, but few are getting saved, fewer disciples are being made, and few are being equipped for ministry. For church leaders in the maintenance culture, none of those issues concern them as long as their attendance is increasing.

For the church to fulfill its mission, it must look beyond the value of attendance to the mission of the church—because the mission is not to draw a big crowd. The mission of the church is to make disciples. The irony is that if the Church would be about the Father's business of making disciples, the Church would experience explosive growth.

### Kingdom-Culture Value: Availability

In the Kingdom-church, we don't just want people attending meetings; we want people available to God to be a divine appointment in someone's life. Believers are available because they have been empowered with the ministry skills and with the heart attitude to be a change agent on the earth. Availability is the heart attitude of stretching our faith and life to impact and change the lives of others around us.

Does your church have the value of attendance or availability?

### Maintenance-Culture Value: Self-Focused

Our Sunday school classes and small groups demonstrate this value when they ask the question: "What do you want to study this quarter?" Why? In the maintenance-culture church, members are only concerned with their needs, and not the needs of others. The question is never asked, "How are we going to fulfill the mission this quarter? How are we going to impact the unsaved this quarter? How are we going to invade the world this quarter? How are we together going to meet someone else's needs? What are we going to do to reach out to the wounded this quarter?" No, in the maintenance culture the only question we have is: "What do we want to do for ourselves this quarter?"

### Kingdom-Culture Value: Needs-Meeting Ministry

Jesus came to meet the needs of those wounded and damaged by the enemy:

> *The Spirit of the Lord is upon Me because He hath anointed Me to preach the gospel to the poor; He hath sent Me to heal the broken-hearted, to preach deliverance to the captives, and recovery of sight to the blind, to set at liberty them that are bruised, to preach the acceptable year of the Lord* (Luke 4:18-19).

The same Jesus lives in you. The same ministry to meet people at their point of need is your ministry, as is showing the same compassion Jesus demonstrated (see Matt. 9:36).

The reason that Jesus, the Anointed One, lives in you is for you to complete the ministry He began, meeting people at their point of need.

Is your church moved with compassion to meet those outside of your church at their point of need? Or are the majority of your members self-focused? Is your church motivated by the maintenance-culture value or the Kingdom-culture value?

### Maintenance-Culture Value: Student

This value can be easily demonstrated by asking members of your church to define a disciple of Jesus. The answer church members give? A disciple is a student. So when they are attending Sunday school class, or reading a Christian book, they are demonstrating what it means to be a disciple of Jesus Christ. There can be no greater passive definition of being a disciple of Jesus Christ than this maintenance-culture definition of a disciple.

A disciple is not a student; a disciple is a follower. Jesus never invited anyone to become a student. He always invited them to follow Him. A disciple is a follower. A student is a sitter.

The maintenance culture is a passive value system that equates knowledge with maturity, instead of action. However, the Bible says that "'knowledge' puffs up, but love builds up" (1 Cor. 8:1 ESV). Maturity and knowledge increase more by doing, not just studying.

*And He saith unto them, Follow Me, and I will make you fishers of men* (Matthew 4:19).

### Kingdom-Culture Value: Disciple-Maker

Jesus said, "Go... and make disciples" (Matt. 28:19 NKJV). We have made that the Great Commission for an institution instead of what it was to Jesus, His mission of life. If Jesus lives in you, His mission has become your mission.

A more literal translation is: "Go, pursue your journey, and make followers." The vision Jesus gives us of His disciples is that they are on the journey to their destiny. They are on the journey following Him, and as they journey, they compel others to join the journey with them.

Those wounded and damaged by satan are lost because they do not know they have a destiny created by God. They do not know the Way (see Acts 9:2) of the journey, so your mission is to compel them to follow you on the journey to their destiny.

Every disciple of Jesus is a disciple-maker, not because of gifting, but because the Jesus who was raised from the dead lives in them. The Jesus who said, "For this purpose I have come...to bear witness to the truth" (John 18:37 ESV), lives in you. That Jesus does not want you to go to a meeting, be nice, and study books. He does not want you to only see the maintenance-culture picture, which is to join a church and become a student in a Sunday school class.

Does your church have the passive maintenance-culture value of church members being students or the dynamic Kingdom-culture value of following Jesus on the journey and compelling others to follow you? Every believer is a leader because every believer is a disciple-maker.

### Maintenance-Culture Value: The Building Church

In the maintenance culture, the church building is the center of church activity. Everything happens at the building. In fact, success of the local church is defined by how many people show up at the building. The weekend attendance at the church building is the church. All the programs are at the church. Everything happens at the church. In the maintenance culture, the word *church* does not identify the biblical Church, the "called-out ones," the people; instead, the church is the building. That is how married the maintenance culture is to the building.

The problem with that is that God is bigger than the church building, and there are more needs outside of the building than inside the building. The Building Church is a very limited vision of the Church, and of God. The mission will never be fulfilled as long as you see your church limited to the Building Church.

### Kingdom-Culture Value: The Kingdom-Church

The Church is not defined by the building where we meet; rather, the biblical Church is defined by relationships. The Kingdom-church value sees your church as bigger—20 times bigger—than your current attendance! God is a big God, and you are part of a big church! The value of the Kingdom-church sees the church as not just our members, but also as the unchurched and unsaved who have relationships with our members.

The Kingdom-church expands beyond the church building and includes those who are not yet saved, not yet part of the Body, but they are part of our vision and mission. Biblically they are identified as the "scattered sheep" (Ezek. 34:12 NKJV). Although they are scattered sheep, they are still our sheep. Only when we have the same compassion on the scattered sheep as we do for the gathered sheep will we ask the questions needed to minister as the Kingdom-church.

Does your church have the small vision of the maintenance-culture Building Church, or does it have the ever-expanding Kingdom-culture value of the Kingdom-church?

### Maintenance-Culture Value: Meetings

The maintenance-culture church believes that its mission is to get Christians to attend meetings. At least it seems that they believe that because they have lots of meetings. The maintenance-culture church defines committed members by how many meetings we can get them to attend. They may not be accomplishing anything; they may not be empowered to live at a higher level; but we have committed members because they attend the meetings.

When I first began the pastorate, I wanted to know who was committed so I increased the number of meetings to attend. What I discovered is that people will give their limited amount of time allotted to church either in meetings or ministry. If the church leaders consume all of their church time in meetings, they will not do ministry. Only have enough meetings to empower for ministry.

The maintenance-culture church finds its value by how many people attend all the meetings. The maintenance culture gets people doing things, talking about things, and accomplishing things for the maintenance-culture church.

That is why we have so many meetings to serve the maintenance-culture church. The meetings do not empower Christians to change anyone outside of the building. The meetings do not engage them in the mission, but they are part of our programs, so therefore, they are serving the church. The maintenance-culture church gets lots of people busy in church business, but not effective in the Father's business. Member burnout is the result of meeting overload in church business. If the church would fulfill the mission, we would be increasing the core worker base instead of expanding the workload by increased attendance.

### Kingdom-Culture Value: Relationships

The Church is not defined by meetings, but by relationships, because relationships release the love of God. People are part of the Body of Christ through loving, heart-fulfilling relationships, not meetings, tasks, or things. Relationships fit us in the Body, hold us in the Body, and supply spiritual needs in the Body (see Eph. 4:16).

Relationships meet the heart fulfillment and life fulfillment needs of people. The people who do not have relationships in your church are not having their needs met. The 20 percent of the members of your church who are doing the 80 percent of the giving and serving are the ones who have relationships. The 80 percent of the people who attend your weekend meetings, but who give and serve only 20 percent, are those who do not have relationships.

Does your church have the value of meetings or relationships?

### Maintenance-Culture Value: "Things Committees"

The maintenance culture spends its time and money on things. It forms committees to talk about things, and its members spend hours talking about projects, tasks, programs—all sorts of *things*.

People on a committee or task force or team spend the vast majority of their time talking about things, not ministering and meeting needs. In the maintenance culture the primary focus is on things, and not people. The committee exists to ensure this part of the maintenance-culture church is done properly. "Things committees" do not accomplish the mission because the purpose of their very existence is to maintain.

### Kingdom-Culture Value: Team Ministry

The purpose of team ministry is to motivate Christians to be more and do more—to stretch themselves to fulfill their destiny. The team is not about making sure the institution is maintained. It is not about programs; the team is about people. It is about the people on the team being encouraged and challenged to get back up in the journey after they've been knocked down.

Team ministry is the motivating structure to encourage disciples to follow the journey and meet others at their point of need by becoming a miracle in their lives. Team ministry is the motivational structure to equip Christians with the support they need to operate at a higher level.

The team has a vision of each one's stretching to a higher level of ministry. It has goals for each one to accomplish, and it has relationships of love to motivate to a higher ministry. The team is the structure for motivation, support, and vision fulfillment.

Does your church have the value of committees or team ministry?

### Maintenance-Culture Value: Nurture

Nurture is the mission of the maintenance-culture church. Every meeting we have is for the purpose of nurture. Sunday school class is to nurture; church service is to nurture; men's meeting nurtures the men and the women's meeting nurtures the women. The teen meeting nurtures the teens, and the singles meeting nurtures the singles. The maintenance culture may have six meetings in a week, but they are all for one purpose: nurture.

The problem with the maintenance-culture value of nurture is that nurturing does not change behavior; it does not equip or empower to live at a higher level. Nurture by its very definition is feeding to sustain the church member to maintain their current level of Christian life.

Nurture enables people to continue living in their fears; it enables them to continue to be controlled by past hurts and wounds. This value does not *change* people; it *enables* people. The maintenance culture is an enabling culture, not an empowering culture.

Nurture enables people to feel good about being mediocre, being less than what Jesus saved them to become in Him. Nurture does not challenge; nurture does not empower; rather, nurture enables.

ᐧ The maintenance-culture church enables church members to live their sub-biblical lives hiding in church, not being changed, not changing their world, and not impacting their world outside of the building.

### Kingdom-Culture Value: Training

Jesus demonstrated this Kingdom-culture value in His relationship with His followers, His disciples. He changed their behavior and lives by training them in the life skills and ministry skills of the Kingdom of Heaven. Training changes behavior. Training empowers disciples to live at a higher level, so the responsibility of the church is to equip disciples with the life skills and ministry skills needed to fulfill their destiny.

The value of training is motivated by faith that the big God in you wants to do something big through you; therefore, we can no longer enable you to sit in church and be less than what God created you to be. You must be trained. You must be equipped so you can fulfill your destiny. You should not miss your destiny simply because your church did not empower you with the life skills, spiritual skills, and ministry skills required for the journey.

Does your church have the value of nurture or training?

### Maintenance-Culture Value: Teacher-Caregiver

The maintenance culture has a vision of the pastor and staff be our teacher-caregivers. In the maintenance-culture church we hire you to teach us the Bible and to care for everyone in the church. The caregiver makes us feel better when we go through difficult times, comforts us when we grieve, and nurtures us through the trials of life. We hire you to maintain our lives the way we are living them.

This vision of the pastor as the teacher-caregiver is not proactive; it is reactive. It reacts to the wishes of the membership of the maintenance-culture church. The question the teacher-caregiver asks is not how to engage the church members to fulfill the mission Jesus gave us. No, the question the teacher-caregiver asks is, "How can I make the people who pay my salary happy?" What makes them happy is maintaining their sub-biblical life.

### Kingdom-Culture Value: Empowering Leadership

The leader of a mission-driven church begins with a vision of the church and the vision of the members at a higher level than what people are living. Therefore, the Kingdom-church pastor sees himself as a pastor-leader. "My role is to lead everyone in my church to a higher level."

Therefore, the pastor of the Kingdom-church has too much love for the disciples to allow them to be stuck maintaining their mediocre sub-biblical lives. He loves them too much to only nurture them, allowing them to miss their destiny. So the pastor-leader sees his mission to empower his members, to model, mentor, train, and teach the required skills to live at a higher level.

The pastor-leader trains his church members to become change-leaders. He believes that the God who created Heaven and earth lives in them, and that big God will do something big through them. Therefore, he refuses to allow them to waste their life in the maintenance culture.

The pastor-leader sees the church as the world's change-agent, which requires leading church members to be their world's change-leaders. The pastor-leader models getting out of his comfort zone and invites his church to get out of their comfort zone. The pastor-leader models making new disciples for Jesus Christ, so his church will follow him and become disciples of the fresh vision, and become disciple makers.

## VALUES CONCLUSION

The maintenance-culture values motivate church members to live a static, uninspiring, passionless life. The Kingdom-culture values motivate disciples to follow the journey to their destiny. Kingdom-culture values motivate men and women of God to lead their members to a higher level, not maintain mediocrity.

The values produce a lifestyle—a quality of life—because they are a vision of life. Either the church exists to maintain mediocrity or the church exists to fulfill the mission and follow the journey.

The question isn't, "What is your retention rate?" The question isn't, "How many people attend your church membership class?" The question is not, "Is your church expanding in attendance?" The questions we ask ourselves should be, "What quality of life is my church producing? How many people in my church are using church to maintain their life, and how many are their world's change-leader? Is our church the world's change agent, or is our church the church member's servant?"

## HOW THE GOOD OF THE MAINTENANCE CULTURE CAUSES YOU TO MISS GOD'S BEST

Here is a story showing how the maintenance-culture values drive the motivation of pastors as well as church members, how they direct the course of the church and outreach events, define the vision of what we are about, and reinforce, or determine, the culture of the church.

I was talking to the church administrator of a church with 800 attendance about the Care Ministry. Whenever I talk with someone like that, I always attempt to discover the "why." Why did the Lord at this time have me in contact with the leadership of the church? I discovered that they had a big opportunity. This was their tenth anniversary of presenting the evangelistic production, "Heaven's Gates and Hell's Flames." I asked him how many responded to the call, and he told me, "Around 400 are saved." I then asked him how many of those actually become part of the church? He first told me that is not their concern; they just want people to be saved and they don't care what church they attend.

I told him I appreciated his open-handed attitude, but the problem is that statistically the people who attend these events seldom, if ever, become disciples—active core workers. Then I asked again how many became part of the church, and he told me between 30 and 50. When he told me how ineffective they were at making disciples, I knew why the Lord had brought us together.

The Lord wanted to join the anointing that is upon the Care Ministries with the church to break through the barriers stopping the church from the harvest the Lord had been providing for nine years. For nine years the devil had been stealing the harvest. The church only knew a meager harvest. The Bible says, "The word of God spread, and the number of the disciples multiplied greatly" (Acts 6:7 NKJV).

This church was oppressed and experiencing not multiplication, but fractional growth—less than 10 percent out of their outreach event! Those results are because of the spiritual barriers upon the church.

I asked him, "If I could show you a way to multiply disciples from 30 to 200, would you be interested?" As I shared the vision and ministry of Care Ministries, he caught it and his faith grew. At the end of our conversation I prayed for them and the harvest at their church.

The next week, after reading my book, *You Are a Miracle—Waiting to Happen!*, he was even more excited. Then he told me they received an unexpected check for several thousands of dollars, and he was putting that in the Care Ministry fund. The Lord had paid for the conference before the board decided to do it. It was obvious by that time that the hand of the Lord was upon this church to release multiplication. The church administrator made his initial presentation to the board, and the response was very positive, especially when they already had the money.

The next week the church administrator told me he would make his final presentation for final approval the following week. He called me to tell me they had a wonderful board meeting and had decided to postpone the Breakthrough Conference. I obviously did not see that as a wonderful board meeting decision, so I asked him why.

He said that before he could ask the board for the final decision, the associate pastor (who would have been over this ministry) had resigned; he had to return to the business world because his family in South America had some sudden and large financial needs. I immediately saw this as an attack from the devil. Jesus told us that the devil comes only to steal, kill, and destroy.

His attack in South America produced lack in the family, produced lack in the church, with the resulting goal of lack in the Father's harvest. The enemy saw this church about to plunder the strongman's house, and he was doing everything he could to protect the goods in his house.

Instead of allowing the church to plunder and steal his good from the kingdom of darkness, the enemy attacked the church by creating a sense of lack, stealing from the church God's opportunity for the greatest harvest in 10 years.

As he told me this story, there arose a faith from within declaring, "No. This harvest is not going to be stolen by the devil's lack. Poverty in the church will not produce poverty in the harvest. That has happened too often." Because I had seen the hand of the Lord, I refused to allow this decision to stand without a fight. I asked the church administrator if he could arrange a phone conference call the following week. At that time the Lord spoke to them to continue on in faith. But the devil had one more way to protect his house from being plundered.

As I prayed for the church and for this wonderful outreach event, the Lord showed me how He wanted to use this church as a model to make disciples and not just decisions. He showed me how to motivate the church members to relationally bond and minister to those who responded, how to motivate the convert back to church the following Sunday to receive baptism and experience immediate relational assimilation. I was ready to return within a week to train 200 people how to make disciples out of the hundreds responding to the Lord.

The Breakthrough Conference was scheduled weeks prior to the production so training could be completed after the conference. The Lord moved upon the congregation of 650 people in the sanctuary and 180 signed up to be part of the Breakthrough Army. They did not provide child care for the afternoon training so I trained only 130, but I knew if they did training on their regularly scheduled Thursday night service, they would be able to train not only the 180, but others would catch the vision and become part of the Breakthrough Army for the great multiplication the Lord had prepared for them.

I set aside time on Monday to consult with the staff and prepare them for the multiplication. I was ready to return and train their members the following Thursday. I had called the airline, putting a ticket on hold to purchase after they agreed to the further training. I knew in my spirit that the Lord had prepared this church at this time for multiplication. Instead of just 30 disciples, they were going to explode with 200. The church was going to break the 1,000 barrier with salvation growth, and the Lord showed me how a second wave of salvations would occur from the first 200 new disciples.

I began the consultation with the vision of 180-200 new disciples and the potential growth of the church and told them there were a few changes that had to be made to achieve those wonderful results. I told them that Thursday night Bible study had to become a training session for the 180 because you cannot suddenly add another meeting to people's schedule and expect people to attend. They have that time allotted to something other than church. If they were going to have a successful training, it had to be done on Thursday night. I had given them a schedule of what needed to be trained for six weeks—three prior and three post decision time—to motivate the church members to make disciples.

The senior pastor had little understanding of the dynamics of what the Lord was about to do. He had not attended the Pastor Leadership School, nor did he attend the Breakthrough Conference training in his church, except for one session and Sunday service.

The enemy had distracted him, and while he had eyes to see, he could not see. He came into the consultation with no vision of what the Lord was about to do, only the vision defined by the maintenance culture from the last nine years. I could tell by his body language that he was not receptive to the idea of changing his teaching/nurturing service into a training session for the volunteer Breakthrough Army to make disciples.

Before he responded, a sister who volunteered for the Care Ministry and was attending the staff meeting exclaimed, "O, Pastor, you can't train on Thursday night! I need your teaching. I have been a member of this church for 25 years, and I love the pastor's teaching. If he taught five times a week, I would be there. He can't train on Thursday night."

After she said that, the senior pastor looked at me as if there was nothing else to say. He then gave me a line I have heard from many pastors who did not want to change for the mission: *"Ken, you do not know our church.* We will conduct the training on Tuesday night."

When I called the following Wednesday to discover how many of the 180 people who were recruited attended the Tuesday training, do you know what number they told me? 48! That was a 78 percent attrition because of the wrong decision. After the production I called to ask what the response was, and they told me they had 400 "saved." Then I asked how many of them made it to church the following Sunday—only 35!

Those were the same results they have been getting for years. Less than 10 percent of the harvest the Lord gave them became members of that church. Once again the fruit fell to the ground. Once again the devil protected his house from being plundered. While the church prays and binds the strongman, without equipping the church and training the members, his house of darkness is safe.

Why did this pastor make the wrong decision? Why was the enemy able to deceive him to miss the visitation of God? Why? He made the wrong choice because he was motivated by maintenance-culture values. He wanted to nurture instead of train; the sister was self-focused instead of giving herself to meet needs. The pastor was afraid that if he trained and did not nurture that attendance would decline at the Thursday service. They disengaged God; He was not big in this pastor's eyes. The maintenance-culture values of a disengaged

God, nurture, self-focus, and attendance drove the decision not to change—and they missed God.

The senior pastor of this wonderful church of 800 missed God because he was motivated by the maintenance-culture values. The course of the evangelistic production was determined by the maintenance-culture values, and the vision of this outreach event was defined by the maintenance-culture values.

The maintenance culture is attractive and has the appearance of being right, so church leaders justify themselves by these values. But it masks the deception that blinds the eyes and dulls the ears of church leaders.

Are the church members primarily self-absorbed with their own struggles? Do they not have the spiritual energy to invest time to pray for others? Is the prayer investment weak? That is the maintenance culture. Often in the maintenance culture there is a spirit of slumber. Church members are too tired to pray and are so consumed with their problems that they are too distracted to care for others. Those symptoms are not normal; they are from a spiritual oppression of darkness in the maintenance-culture church.

There is "interference" to the spiritual reception to hear what the Lord would say to us because of the background noise of church member's fears, discouragement, and feelings of guilt and unworthiness to be a miracle. Maintenance-culture church members are unaware of God speaking to them. They do not hear the Lord through counsel. Often, it seems like there is a spiritual short circuit because the strength of the Spirit is not available for spiritual things. This culture prohibits investment in the things of the Spirit.

This condition is frustrating to pastors, and they often confide to me a sense that what they are saying may be heard, but it is not heeded by the members. Do not blame the pastor or church leadership if you discover your church is in this suppressive spirit in the maintenance-culture prison. They are as much a victim of its deception as anyone else.

In this spiritual environment church folks tend to be drawn to think negatively about themselves and others. They have a general sense of wanting more and not getting it, and feeling like there is something wrong with the church service that is the source of their oppressed feeling. Often people blame the church for this spiritual lack.

In the maintenance-culture church, folks don't have the desire to invest more in the things of the Spirit, while at the same time they want God to help them more than He does. Church members don't see that they need to change, but they sure do want their circumstances to change.

In the maintenance-culture fog, their analysis is, "I'm doing all right; I'm doing about what other members of the church are doing." The "church member comparative analysis" is flawed because 95 percent of the church members are unknowingly oppressed under the maintenance culture.

They see no correlation between their problems and the weak reception to the Spirit, or tepid response to the Spirit. In the maintenance culture, they do not connect the dots between their lack of investment in their relationship with God and the feeling of lack in their life. Yet no one talks of a hunger for God. We are too busy.

The maintenance culture blinds the eyes of our heart so we vaguely see darkened images in the fog of our unbelief. When we seek God for answers, we see dimly and hear faintly so we do not know the source of our dissatisfaction. We don't know why we don't know.

*Do you or your church have the maintenance-culture standards of success?*

- You think that an increase in attendance and budget is success, but do not know how many new disciples the church has made.

- You are satisfied that there is an increase in Sunday school attendance, but few are trained in life and ministry skills to impact others with God.

*Does your church have the maintenance-culture church statistics?*

- Approximately 98 percent of the growth of your church is from people who are already Christians.

- Around 95 percent of your members are barren and fearful of the mission to make disciples.

- Only 2 percent of your busyness is invested in the Mission.

- Are you one of the 95 percent who have not made a disciple?

### Does your church have the maintenance-culture symptoms?

- The staff spends most of its time on maintaining church programs and members.

- Many members lack passion for the mission.

- The members are too busy to serve.

- Over 80 percent of your attenders are non-core workers.

- The board spends almost all time and money to maintain church facilities, church members, and church programs.

### Does your church have the maintenance-culture results?

- Retention of Christian visitors is only 10 percent to 20 percent.

- Assimilation of all of your visitors is only 1 percent to 5 percent.

- You only have a few people recruited for your future church.

### Do you have the maintenance-culture values?

- Do you only attend church, or are you available to be a divine appointment on Sunday?

- Is God disengaged from your life, or is He doing big things in your life?

- Are you only a student or are you a disciple-maker?

- Is your testimony limited to being nice, or are you empowered for ministry?

- Do you go to meetings, but don't have good relationships in church?

- Do you study the Word, but are not trained in ministry and life skills to live at a higher level?

- Do you see your church as those in the Building Church, or do you see your church as big as God does—the Kingdom-church?

- Do you have a Building Church or a Kingdom-church?

- Is God disengaged, or is He a big God in your church?

## ARE YOU IMPRISONED IN THE MAINTENANCE CULTURE?

The apostle Peter was imprisoned in his maintenance culture. He faced a seemingly impossible situation. In Acts chapter 12, King Herod killed John, the brother of James, then had Peter arrested and placed in prison to kill him after Passover season. Not only was this an impossible situation for Peter, but for the entire church.

This was the darkest hour the church had encountered. King Herod had the entire church under his power. Satan's scheme was to use King Herod to destroy this young church before it had a chance to grow stronger, to be the alternative Kingdom-culture on the earth. He would kill the church leadership to deflate the faith of the people then scatter them like sheep without a shepherd.

Peter was now in an impossible situation. There was no hope for escape. Herod had ordered 16 soldiers to keep Peter in that prison cell. He had two soldiers at his cell door, and two soldiers were in the cell, one chained to his right hand and one chained to his left hand. In the natural realm, it was an impossible situation. There was no escaping this prison. No escaping certain death. No escaping the church's becoming an insignificant sect of Messianic Jews with no leaders. Satan's schemes were working as he planned. The evil forces of darkness were eager to crush this rebellion in their dark kingdom.

The American Church is in an equally impossible situation. Satan has imprisoned the church in the darkness of the maintenance-culture prison. Experts say the church cannot change and will always remain in the maintenance culture. We can only cope with the condition, and allow the church to become an insignificant sect in American life.

## TWO RESPONSES TO DARKNESS

*Peter therefore was kept in prison:* **but prayer was made without ceasing** *of the church unto God for him. And when Herod would have brought him forth, the same night* **Peter was sleeping** *between two soldiers, bound with two chains: and the keepers before the door kept the prison* (Acts 12:5-6).

Some key things to notice here are:

• Peter was sleeping.

• Prayer was made without ceasing.

## PETER WAS SLEEPING

Why was Peter sleeping the night before he was to be killed by the sword? Why didn't he, like Paul (in Acts 16:26), praise God in the darkness of the prison? The eyes of his mind were blinded by the god of this world (see 2 Cor. 4:4). He saw the natural circumstances of the prison walls, the oppressive darkness of the prison, and the soldiers that were bound to his hands. The facts were just too overwhelming to think that anything but death awaited him. Peter believed what he saw. It was logical. It was accurate. There was no escape.

John the Baptist did not have a miraculous deliverance from prison. He was killed by a man who thought of himself as a god. There was no reasoning with this self-serving politician who killed people for his benefit. So why would he let Peter go free? Peter believed what he saw, and he slumbered in the unbelief of sight. He resigned himself to his circumstances. He resigned himself at this critical moment to walk by sight, and not by faith. Why pray for deliverance? Why praise God in the darkness of this prison?

The circumstances convinced Peter that the situation was impossible. Since it was obvious he was going to die, Peter slept because he saw impossible circumstances. Spiritual slumber occurs when you quit praying, quit praising God, quit believing. He was not just resting; he was in spiritual slumber. At the moment he needed to be praying for God's salvation, he was sleeping. The moment he needed to be praising God and rejoicing in all things, he was sleeping. The moment the eyes of faith would have been looking for God to move, he was sleeping.

That is the one common behavior of the maintenance culture: sleeping. Instead of "stretching" our prayer time, we spend little time in prayer. Instead of stretching our prayers into impossible, stretching prayers into the night, we are sleeping. Jesus said we will either faint or pray (see Luke 18:1). Many in the maintenance culture are like Peter; they have fainted and are in spiritual slumber.

Often church members feel they are imprisoned with no hope. They resign themselves to the prison of the maintenance culture. The devil, the god of this world, has deceived the minds of those who do not believe (see 2 Cor. 4:4). Through that deception he has imprisoned you in the prison of the maintenance culture of your church. His scheme is to kill your ministry, steal your anointing, and destroy your destiny. That is why the thief has you in the maintenance-culture prison.

Why are pastors so oppressed with discouragement and disillusionment? They see the limitations of the maintenance-culture prison walls. They are blinded by the darkness of the prison, so they do not have the spiritual sight to see the vision and work of the Holy Spirit.

A spirit of fear (see 2 Tim. 1:7) is chained to the right hand of the anointing, and a spirit of discouragement (see Isa. 61:3) is chained to the left hand of spiritual authority, limiting the results only to the efforts of man, and the results of the arm of flesh. The very power and authority needed to break through the prison wall that oppresses cannot be exercised because they are bound to spiritual forces who gain their strength from past negative experiences in the prison of the maintenance culture. Fearful prayer won't change anything. The fears from my past become the harvest of my future. Unbelief becomes reality in the prison of the maintenance culture.

Peter was sleeping because he was imprisoned, not in the Roman cell, but in the prison of the maintenance culture. He was no longer on mission; he was no longer on the journey; he was maintaining his life until what he saw would come to pass. Peter was deceived into thinking the reality of his sight was the finality of the work of God.

I will not deny the *reality* of the circumstances, but I will deny the *finality*. It is not final until God moves. Your testimony of God's greatness is seen best with the backdrop of your darkest moment. Your miracle in the dark prison will only happen when your faith moves you to engage the weapons mighty before God for the casting down of strongholds (see 2 Cor. 10:4).

The impossible circumstance was a product of Peter's fear-activated imagination. The only way Peter could conclude his life was over was to imagine it. He did not see it. It was not final. He allowed his imagination to be activated by fear. His fear cast a vision of defeat and doom for him. His fear-activated imagination led him to the place of discouragement and fainting so that he was spiritually inactive—slumbering in the prison of his unbelief. The maintenance culture is the product of our own fear-activated imagination.

Instead of allowing the Spirit of God to activate our imagination with faith, we allow the spirit of fear to activate our imagination with fear of the circumstances we see. Instead of seeing by faith, we see the natural and allow the enemy through fear and unbelief to interpret what is going to take place with what we see.

The maintenance culture is a prison where you walk by sight and not by faith.

The maintenance-culture prison is when the god of this world blinds the eyes of the minds of those who do not believe.

### *The maintenance culture is the prison of deception:*

- To walk by sight and not by faith.

- Walking by sight produces natural men (see 1 Cor. 2:14) doing natural things.

- Walking, living, by sight produces fear of failure.

- The sight produces discouragement.

- Fear and discouragement produce a weak, fainting, and soft soul.

- Spiritual slumber is the result of not having the strength of the Spirit.

- Lack of strength produces disengagement from the battle.

- Not battling in spiritual warfare produces defeated lives.

*How do you know if you are imprisoned in the maintenance culture of life?*

- Are you easily discouraged?

- Are you fearful and insecure?

- Are you satisfied with maintaining your life?

- Are you afraid of change?

- Are you having difficulty investing time in prayer?

- Are you having difficulty praising God in all things?

- Are you having difficulty hearing God, which creates faith in your heart?

If so, you are imprisoned in the maintenance culture.

The battle in the spiritual realm against the enemy is never fought—at least not by you—so you continue to experience poverty and lack. Until faith-filled words are employed in the battle, the enemy will continue to have authority over your ministry, church, and business.

Spiritual slumber is the behavior of limited prayer, praise, and intercession. The board invests little time interceding for anything beyond the immediate decisions they must make. There is little opportunity for God to answer prayer because no one is praying. When men of God slumber in unbelief, God can't do the impossible when He wants to because He cannot answer prayer that is never uttered.

Praise cannot open doors if it is never sung (see Acts 16:25-26). Profession cannot conquer the enemy if never spoken out in faith (see 1 Sam. 17). The prayer of faith cannot be answered if you are not before God (see James 5:15).

Proclamation cannot set at liberty the oppressed (see Luke 4:18) without speaking the good news. The weapons for our warfare, which are mighty before God for the casting down of strongholds (see 2 Cor. 10:4), cannot be effective if they are not employed.

Spiritual slumber causes us to not perceive the enemy, nor see the need to engage the spiritual weapons. The first value that motivates the behavior in the maintenance-culture church is "God is disengaged." God is disengaged because we do not pray, and God cannot move. A disengaged God is the result of a slumbering church.

We slumber in discouragement. We slumber in unbelief. We sleep in self-doubt. We sleep in worry. The very moment that demands spiritual engagement of prayer, we sleep in the unbelief of the inevitability of what we see with the natural eye as the inevitability of satan's plans for our life—death—just as Peter thought his death was inevitable. John the Baptist was killed; God did not deliver him. No miracle for John so why should there be a miracle for me?

Peter had every reason to believe in the outcome as satan desired. "Look at the 16 soldiers guarding me. Look at my chains bound to my hands and bound to the two guards in this prison cell with me. Look at the prison and the locked prison door. There is not any way for me to get out of this prison. It is impossible for me to get out of here."

How many times do we look at the evil he has cast upon us in the natural circumstances, then agree with the devil's declaration, "This is impossible. I cannot be delivered from this circumstance." Instead of doing battle, we resign ourselves to what we see, agree with the devil, the father of lies and a thief, then slumber in the deceptive darkness of the maintenance culture.

The eyes of the mind have been blinded by the darkness of unbelief. We lay in the maintenance-culture prison cell paralyzed with fear—fear of failing if we attempt to do something great for God. So we resign ourselves to the mediocrity of the maintenance culture.

This is the condition of the maintenance-culture church. Many Christians have resigned themselves to just being members of the church. They have no sense of mission or passion, so they slumber in the maintenance-culture church prison. They have quit believing, quit leading, quit praying for the Spirit of God to invade their lives.

Many wonderful Christians in the maintenance-culture church are no longer challenged to follow Christ to their destiny. They are enabled through unbelief no longer to search for the higher ways and higher plans of God. They look for someone who is hungry to go higher in their destiny, but find only campers on the side of the journey. Many are slumbering in the maintenance culture—the culture of mediocrity, convenience, and barrenness.

The flame of passion has been stolen from the hearts of those who once were excited about the things of God. Oppressed by the limitations in the maintenance-culture church prison, they resign themselves to conduct church business, instead of pursuing the transcending vision of the Kingdom-church.

## PRAYING FOR THE IMPOSSIBLE

*Peter therefore was kept in prison: but prayer was made without ceasing of the church unto God for him* (Acts 12:5).

You don't have to resign yourself to church business in the natural realm, playing the game of church politics, defending your territory, winning at the expense of others losing. The ways of man in the maintenance-culture church are temporal. Although they may provide your soul with a sense of importance, the significance that comes from the Kingdom cannot be experienced in the maintenance culture. The ways of God in the Kingdom-church transcend the ways of man and lift us to our destiny.

The departure point out of the maintenance-culture church and the entrance into the ways of God in the Kingdom of Heaven is prayer. The Kingdom of Heaven is where man loses control to enter into the ways of God, where God accomplishes the impossible when He is in control. The Jerusalem church understood the need for God to gain control of this impossible situation, because only He can do the impossible. They made "constant prayer" without ceasing to the Lord.

The word translated "constant" is a medical word for stretching your muscle. Why would Luke the physician use this word when writing this account of Peter's imprisonment? Luke equated exercising and stretching muscles with the spiritual muscle of prayer. The more you exercise prayer, the more powerful it is. The more you train your prayer muscle, the more effective it is.

Prayer and faith are spiritual muscles that only get stronger with use. "Only through resistance does strength come" is a principle every weight lifter understands. When we just maintain our lives and fall into spiritual slumber, our faith muscles and prayer muscles become atrophied. The maintenance culture is destructive because in it there is no need to stretch our prayers into the impossible. Maintenance is possible, not impossible. There is no stretching of our prayers into the night watches. Maintenance requires only a little prayer and weak faith; therefore spiritual muscles become atrophied.

The early Church stretched their prayer muscle and their faith muscle into the realm of the impossible. Confronted with the impossible situation, they prayed without ceasing; they stretched their time in prayer and they stretched their faith through prayer.

## GOD INVADED THE IMPOSSIBLE WITH HIS ANGEL

*And* [the angel] *raised him up, saying, Arise up quickly. And his chains fell off from his hands* (Acts 12:7).

Because the church stretched their prayers and stretched their faith muscles to receive the impossible, God sent an angel to deliver Peter from his prison. Now when the angel came, he was not necessarily kind to Peter. The word translated as "smote" in this passage was used nine other times in the Bible. In eight of those instances people were either wounded or died from being smitten. The picture then is that the angel slapped Peter up across the head and commanded, "Arise quickly!" Then the spiritual angel grabbed him and physically raised Peter off the bed of slumber in that prison cell. When Peter rose up out of slumber, the Bible says "his chains fell off of his hands."

The description of the chains that bound Peter's hands was not "the" chains, but "his" chains. How did these chains become Peter's personal chains? He allowed the past experience of John the Baptist's execution, the 16 soldiers assigned to his bondage, the prison darkness, and the chains to determine his future. His soul slumbered because it was captive to the circumstances in unbelief. The chains that shackled Peter bound his hand of Kingdom anointing and his hand of Kingdom authority. His fear fragmented his thinking so he could not believe. His discouragement diffused his will so he could not pray. Peter was bound not only by physical chains, but his soul was bound by what his flesh saw. He saw by the eyes of flesh instead of the eyes of faith, and he slumbered.

Spiritual chains bind our hands of Kingdom anointing and Kingdom authority, rendering us incapable of binding the strongman. Instead of us binding, conquering, and plundering the strongman's house, spirits of fear and discouragement bind our right hand of Kingdom anointing and the left hand of Kingdom authority. We must first have the chains fall off our hands so the anointing will destroy the yoke and spiritual authority will bind in Heaven what has been bound on earth (see Matt. 18:18).

The spiritual force delegated to the Kingdom-church by King Jesus to expand His Kingdom on earth through multiplication of disciples is imprisoned and chained to slumbering, bound, and barren church members in the maintenance culture. The Kingdom-church in Jerusalem, however, had no such limitations. Their hands were free to be raised in praise to God. Their hearts were free to believe God to be in control for the impossible. Their tongues were free to profess the deliverance of God. They stretched their faith-activated imagination into the realm of the impossible—the ways of God—and prayed for Peter's freedom. They stretched their season of prayer beyond a short morning devotional into hours of desperate prayer to see God invade the impossible with His deliverance. They were the Kingdom-church because their prayers brought the Kingdom of Heaven to earth.

The church imprisoned in the maintenance culture will never be the Kingdom-church because it does not have the spiritual capacity to exercise prayer and faith to bring the Kingdom of Heaven to earth.

## Do You Need Institutional Change or Individual Transformation?

I invited a pastor friend to my Maximize Your Church conference, and his response was, "I will do that in two years because my denomination has begun a program in our district." He was very excited about this program that was to change the culture by having a vision committee evaluating several different aspects of church programs to determine which program was the weakest, then develop a two-year plan to increase the effectiveness of the church.

I asked him what the desired end result of this two-year church-changing program was. My friend told me, "Each church would define their own expectations." When he said that I realized this church-changing program would be 100 percent successful. This church-changing program will consume two years of church members' time as they evaluate their church from the values of the maintenance culture, and they will still be in the maintenance culture after two years because they have not changed their values nor their vision of the church. The natural man will look at the natural church and arrive at the end of the time frame where they began—in the maintenance culture. Their programs may be improved and they will do a better job of their church business, but their results for the Kingdom and the Father's business will be little changed. Since biblical standards will be ignored as they set their own definition of success, they will feel very successful in the maintenance culture. It will be a feel-good exercise, for both the church members and the kingdom of darkness. Neither will be changed.

The American church's approach to culture change is institutional: Identify and improve the institution's 7 to 12 (depending upon which expert you follow) core services and programs. This culture change model is what the business world does, and the church follows the business world. Then, to make sure everyone feels good about what they do, let each church define their own expectations.

Institutional culture change will not transform the church from the maintenance culture to the Kingdom-culture. The source of the maintenance culture is not the 7 or 12 programs or services—it is the church member.

## CHURCH CULTURE CHANGE IS NOT THE RESULT OF INSTITUTIONAL CHANGE, BUT INDIVIDUAL TRANSFORMATION

To understand how the church's culture can be changed, you first must understand how the church culture became a maintenance culture. The definition of culture is: "the act of developing the intellectual and moral faculties of the members of a specific group."

Let me give you an example. The elite of this country—the folks who live in South Hampton, who have the old money, the aristocrats—have a strongly developed culture produced by their education system. They send their children to the proper preschools to prepare them for their culture. Then their children attend the prestigious grade and prep schools, to be accepted to the elite colleges, so the end product will be a cultured person—someone who knows how to behave in this elite circle of society.

This education process begins with an end in mind, a vision of what a socially elite person sounds like, acts like, dresses like, and does, then develops the educational process to fulfill the vision of the member of the elite society. The cultural education process begins with a vision of the member of the culture.

Culture development begins with a vision of what a member of that culture is to be and do, then educates the members to fulfill the vision. Here is another example. Secular humanists have had a vision of the United States' culture as a godless culture. They developed our nation's educational system to produce a godless generation. It is not an accident that the culture of the United States has changed; it was intentional, purposeful. The maintenance-culture church did not confront the humanist culture because the humanist godless culture did not interfere with the church's vision and culture development.

The maintenance-culture church has a vision of what a member of its culture sounds like, acts like, and dresses like. The maintenance-culture church does not have a vision of the society in which it exists. What is this vision of the maintenance culture that is developed by the maintenance-culture education?

The vision of the maintenance culture is a *church member*.

## WHAT DOES A CHURCH MEMBER DO?

*A church member:*

- *Attends the meetings of the church*
- *Serves the programs of the church*
- *Fellowships with the members in the church*
- *Gives to the needs of the church*

A *good* church member, gives more, attends more, serves more, and fellowships more.

Being a good church member, in the maintenance culture, does not include the mission that King Jesus died for us to fulfill. That is why secular humanists could develop a godless culture in our nation with no opposition from the maintenance-culture church. The two cultures could coexist. If the church had the Kingdom-culture, the church would have been invasive in the humanist culture, confronted it, and won the cultural war with the secular humanist.

## ATTENDING A MAINTENANCE-CULTURE CHURCH WILL PRODUCE A MAINTENANCE-CULTURE LIFESTYLE

Maintain your Christian life, maintain your family to be Christian churchgoers, and maintain your church programs to maintain your family. That is the vision of the maintenance-culture church member.

It is the family that serves in the nursery when their children are in the nursery; then when their kids graduate to children's church, they serve in the children's church; then when their kids are teens they work with the teens. They serve to maintain. That is the vision of a good church member, and we applaud that level of commitment. They are good church members, and we wish everyone was as faithful as they are.

How does a good church member behave? They are nice and non-invasive with those who are not members of the church. They won't confront evil; rather, they will turn the other cheek. They will tolerate secular humanists defining the American culture as godless as long as they let us be good church members and raise our family to be good churchgoers in our church buildings.

The attitude is that when non-members, visitors, and strangers attend our church, we will be friendly to them too, but since we don't know them, and they are not part of "us," that is the only response and responsibility to them. My culture defines and limits who I invest my time and energy in—the church.

Church members protect their territory in the maintenance-culture church. The maintenance-culture vision of the church is the "Building

Church." It is a very limited, small, and myopic vision of the church. Maintenance-culture church members are motivated by fear to protect their little territory. They feel like, "I must protect my space, my classroom, my time, my program." In the maintenance-culture church, members control the small things and lose the big thing—their destiny.

"After all, I am so busy. I am busy at work. I am busy with my family. I am busy at church. I am just busy, busy, busy. I am too busy to get anyone saved. Anyway, I'm not an evangelist; I took a test." Maintenance-culture church members excuse themselves from the life of mission. They repeat this excuse as a mantra from hell. The church member misses the moment when Jesus passes by because they are unavailable to follow Him. They are just too busy.

Recently I was at dinner with a minister who made this statement, "People are so busy. There is nothing wrong with it; that's just the way it is." That is the view of church members through the prism of the maintenance culture. Although that is the way it is, there is plenty wrong with satan stealing the time dedicated to God. When the God-dedicated time is offered to the idols of mammon, entertainment, and things of this world, not only is the Lord offended, but the Kingdom of Heaven cannot come to earth. The soulish ways of man cannot be identified as sins of the flesh, but the end result is the same.

Maintenance-culture church members allocate their time to "serve the church," and that is all the time King Jesus receives from us. Somehow, we miss the connection that if we give Him only limited time, then we are not giving Him lives, He does not have our hearts, and we miss the abundance and multiplication He has for us.

You can be a really good church member—attend the meetings of the church, serve the programs of the church, give to the needs of the church, and fellowship with the members of the church—but have absolutely nothing to do with the mission King Jesus died for: your mission of life. Statistically, 9.5 responsible church members out of 10 do not fulfill the mission of a disciple of the anointed King Jesus because it is not part of their culture—maintenance culture. When a person attends church, serves church, fellowships in the church, and gives to the church, the church business has disengaged them from the ministry.

The maintenance-culture church member camps out on the side of the breakthrough journey, never seeing the heights the Lord will lift them to if they will only say yes to Him. They are so busy with church business that they do not see the Father's business.

Millions of church members are really good church members, but do not have a mission for their life. They are not fulfilling the mission Jesus died for. They do not have a vision for their life; rather, they allow the culture to lead them into a mediocre life maintaining their church. The maintenance-culture attitude leads you to an altitude of mediocrity instead of the altitude of miracles.

- Maintenance culture is the way of man. It is the natural man attempting to do the things of God. It is using God to gratify the soul of man. It is the death of both the people in the church and the church.

- Maintenance-culture church members:

  - *Beat themselves up (guilt).*

  - *Put themselves down (discouragement).*

  - *Are fearful of going beyond their comfort zone.*

  - *Produce behavior that causes them to miss the best God has for them.*

In farming there is a term called the "hard pan." The hard pan is developed over a period of time when the farmer sets the plow down only so far and no deeper. Underneath that plowed ground develops earth as hard as cement. What I discovered in the maintenance culture was that I repented only so deep. I repented of the obvious sins, but underneath were attitudes that quenched the Spirit of God. The problem was that I could justify the wrong attitudes with right thinking. The only way to know the hard pan in your heart is by asking the Holy Spirit to reveal it to you.

The hard pan in the maintenance culture is the attitude of being satisfied with being a church member, and not hungry to be like King Jesus. There is nothing wrong with being a church member, but if your vision of what it means to follow Jesus is only to be a church member, you will remain in the maintenance culture.

Right now light is shining in the darkness of your maintenance-culture prison. This moment, the angel of the Lord is saying to you, "Arise quickly!" The light of this truth is shining into the darkness of your maintenance-culture prison. You don't have to be imprisoned any longer; you don't have to be bound any longer. Your chains will fall off your hands if you will wake up, shake the dust of the maintenance culture off yourself, arise, and follow the angel out of the prison.

This is your moment to become like King Jesus by joining me on the breakthrough journey. I have been in the maintenance culture. I have seen how it has robbed me of God's best. I know there is not fresh anointing in the maintenance culture because I have gone down that road. I have thought I did not need to change. I have refused to change, and I have missed the times of refreshing, missed it so many times. I will never go back to the maintenance culture of mediocrity again. I will never go back to the life that is satisfied with less than becoming like King Jesus. The flame of passion died in my soul for lack of fresh breath of God. I have experienced all the lies.

I am inviting you in the tender mercies of God to join me on the journey. Don't stay in the stale slumber and boring life in the maintenance culture. No longer give fear and discouragement the authority to lead you in the path of mediocrity. Repent today. Repent out of the maintenance culture, so you can follow King Jesus into the fullness of His Kingdom-church.

When God called you, a work of the Spirit of God occurred in your heart to have passion for the things of God. A fire burned in your heart to kick in the gates of hell and bring the Kingdom of Heaven to earth. The maintenance culture sucks the breath of God out of the board meetings, out of the Sunday school classes, out of the small groups, and out of church itself. There is no fresh anointing; there is no passion, only maintenance. There is no sense of bringing Heaven to earth, only surviving on earth.

When you said yes to Jesus' becoming the Lord of your life, you did not intend for it to end in the maintenance culture. You are not following Jesus to maintain. You do not want to live the remainder of your

Christian life with no passion, no vision, no mission—asleep in the maintenance culture.

This is a picture of you and your church. You are oppressed under the barrier of the maintenance culture. The spiritual forces of fear, discouragement, unbelief, disappointment, and defeat in the past are pushing on you to stay under this spiritually oppressive and depressing barrier.

You must break through the barrier! You must not allow the spiritual forces of evil to keep you from your destiny and God's blessing. It is time to break through today!

How do you break through the maintenance-culture barrier?

Jesus commanded us, "Repent, for the kingdom of heaven is at hand" (Matt. 4:17 NKJV).

You have a choice to continue in the natural ways of man in the maintenance culture church, or repent into the Kingdom-church. I can hear the objections now: "But I am serving the Kingdom when I serve my church!"

- When churches grow, but do not expand the Kingdom of God, the maintenance-culture church has little if anything to do with Kingdom-church.

- When God's people become imprisoned in the maintenance-culture church, allowing satan to steal their inheritance and destiny away from them, it is not Kingdom-church.

- When members are maintained in the church building, but victims are not delivered out of darkness, it is not Kingdom-church.

- When followers of Christ are enabled maintain a lifestyle tormented by their fears, defeated by their past, and burdened with their guilt, that is not the Kingdom church.

The maintenance-culture church is satan's counterfeit to the Kingdom-church. The maintenance-culture church minimizes your influence by keeping you imprisoned. King Jesus wants to release you to maximize your influence for the transcendent Kingdom of Heaven.

The Lord has a promise for those who hunger and thirst. This is not a message of condemnation, but a message of hope: A fresh move of the Spirit is coming to the church. A fresh anointing is coming upon you.

How do you receive the fresh anointing? How does the church receive a fresh breath of God? Repent! Change! Leave the static stale state of the maintenance-culture church member camping out on the side of the journey to God's vision and destiny. Join the journey to a higher level. You can break through the barriers that have restricted your life. Your hands do not have to be bound any longer. You can free your right hand for Kingdom anointing and your left hand for Kingdom authority. You can maximize your influence to change your life, change your church, and change your world. If you do not change yourself, you cannot maximize your life. When you change, then you have the capacity to be a change leader like King Jesus.

You can change your life. You can change your church. You can change your world by the power of the Spirit of God. It may look impossible, but Peter was in an impossible situation, and the Lord God invaded His impossible circumstance with the Spirit of the living God.

First, leave the maintenance culture by repenting from being just a church member, and then become like King Jesus, the world's change-leader.

Here is the promise from the Father:

*Repent* [change your mind] *therefore and be converted* [change your behavior], *that your sins may be blotted out, so that times of refreshing may come from the presence of the Lord* (Acts 3:19 NKJV).

God promises not just one time, but time after time after time of refreshing. How do you receive time after time of refreshing? Repent time after time. Each time you change, the Spirit of God is there with a fresh anointing in your life.

- Fresh move of the Spirit

- Fresh anointing

- Breakthrough anointing

This message is not about how bad the church is, or how weak church members may be. It is about a promise from the Father that He yearns to honor in each one of us. The promise from the Father is times of refreshing—time after time after time. The Lord yearns to give you a fresh anointing more than you want to receive it.

What qualifies you for the promise of times of refreshing? The fresh anointing is for all who will qualify themselves. You do not have to be knowledgeable; you do not need to be spiritual. You only need to be thirsty and hungry enough to change, to repent.

What qualifies you for a fresh anointing in your life? Change!

Church members in the maintenance culture do not experience times of refreshing because they do not see why they need to change. In fact, many in the maintenance culture do not like change. They view change as loss and get angry. Those who are hungry for God want to change because change is the qualification for a fresh anointing in our lives.

When we change our minds and change our behavior, we qualify for a fresh anointing. The time we need the anointing is when we come to a moment of resistance in our lives. We come to that point when we must decide, "Am I going to change or continue to live as I have in the past? Am I going to continue to allow fear to control my behavior? Am I going to continue to allow discouragement to weaken my resolve? Am I going to continue to allow guilt to disqualify me from the blessings of God?"

The moments when resistance turns into a refusal to change are when the enemy draws us away from the journey. He distracts us from our mission. Every moment is a lost moment when we refuse to change to become like King Jesus who saw by faith and was moved with compassion, sensitive to the wounds of others, instead of leading a self-absorbed life.

When church members in the maintenance culture do not change, do not like change, and refuse change, they declare by their actions that they see themselves as having arrived and are already just like Jesus. Even though under the hard pan of their heart they are troubled with fears, their mind is filled with worry and doubt, and their behavior is self-focused, their resistance to change declares that they have arrived. They may not smoke or cuss, but their soul is tormented by the forces of darkness because in the maintenance culture you cannot receive times of refreshing; there is no fresh anointing because there is no change, only maintenance.

I know. I have been in the maintenance culture. I have refused to change because I did not need to change. I listened to the voices that distracted me from the journey. I camped out. King Jesus came passing by and I did not care. I was not going on; I did not need to.

The worst place to be is in the maintenance culture allowing the enemy to distract you when King Jesus passes by. You miss divine visitation after divine visitation—but you are unaware King Jesus was there.

But if, at that moment of resistance, you doubt your doubts and believe the promise that God is your Rewarder (see Heb. 11:6), then the moment of resistance becomes a moment of refreshing as the break-through anointing comes fresh upon you to empower you to pursue the journey. Everyday moments of resistance become moments of refreshing as we continually say yes to King Jesus, yes to faith, yes to hope, yes to the love of the Father, yes to the journey that transforms us to be like King Jesus, ruling in the midst of our enemies.

Each day you have opportunities to change, to repent, and to move upward in the journey to your destiny. Each day, if you choose to allow the background noise of fear, self-doubt, and disappointment to distort the voice of God to be a sounding brass, a clanging cymbal, then, at those moments, you invite the resistor to quench the very anointing available to break through. Those moments in which you choose not to change are moments of missing God's best, bound in the maintenance culture.

For many church members those moments of resistance have become years of maintenance without change, maintenance without going higher—years convincing ourselves we cannot go higher; years of listening to the fears that control our relationships, control our behavior; years of allowing the disappointments of the past, the wounds from the sins of others, to control our future. Maintenance is all we know. Maintaining is what church members do, excusing the life of mediocrity, becoming judgmental of those who refuse to maintain. Moments become years, years become a lifestyle, and a lifestyle becomes a culture.

What is the alternative to being a church member? Be like Jesus— King Jesus the change-leader of the world!

*King Jesus, I confess to You that I have been imprisoned in the maintenance culture in my life. I hunger for the ways of God that are higher than my ways. I thirst for a fresh anointing in my life. I repent of the maintenance culture. I want to fulfill my destiny. I want to become the vision You had of me when You created me. I refuse to live anything less than Your vision of me.*

*I follow Your messenger today. I see the light of how my life has been imprisoned, how the anointing and authority has been bound. I don't want that any longer. I change my mind about the path I am following.*

*I repent, change my mind, from being just a church member. I see how there is more for me. I want to be like King Jesus.*

*I will turn, change my direction, this day. I no longer follow the path to barrenness in the maintenance culture. I begin the breakthrough journey today. I declare I will become the vision God has of me. I will not settle for less than my creative purpose. I am going to a higher level. I will break through the past experiences that have wounded my soul. I will break through the circumstantial barriers that seem to stop me.*

*I am no longer part of the maintenance culture. I have joined the Kingdom-culture on the earth. I hunger for Your purposes to be revealed in my life. I thirst for a fresh anointing to empower me to live at a higher level.*

*In the name, authority, and office of King Jesus, Amen.*

# 7

# Vision Will Maximize Your Influence

To have the power to break through the barriers of the maintenance culture that are marginalizing your life, you must live a different kind of life. To live that different kind of life you must life by vision. To maximize your influence you must have God's vision of you. Energized by God's vision, you will break through the barriers upon your soul to maximize your life! You will learn the principles of living by vision, then you will catch the vision of being like Jesus—King Jesus.

Faith in the future gives power to the present:

*Being confident of this very thing, that He which hath begun a good work in you will perform it until the day of Jesus Christ* [the Anointed King Jesus] (Philippians 1:6).

God loves you so much. He loves you just the way you are, yet God loves you too much to leave you the way you are. God is the God of the second chance. You may have gone through the worst failure imaginable, but God isn't finished with you yet. You may have made the biggest blunder the world has ever seen, but God is not finished with you yet. You may look into your future and see only darkness, but God is not finished with you yet. You may even think your life has little value, but God isn't finished with you yet!

You have a future because God has a vision of you. You have a future because God began a good work in you. You have a future because God doesn't quit on you; He believes in you when you do not believe in yourself. He knows what He put in you. He knows the awesome life He created you to live. He knows the adventures waiting for you. He knows the miracles He has already planned for you. He only needs one thing from you. Get on the journey. The journey to your maximized life begins right now—the beginning of your maximized life is vision.

**Your future will not be determined by your past experiences.**

**Your future will not be determined by your present circumstances.**

**Your future will be determined by your vision!**

*Where there is no vision the people perish...* (Proverbs 29:18).

There are four alternate translations for "perish":

1. When there is no vision, people are *unmotivated.*

2. When there is no vision, people are *undisciplined.*

3. When there is no vision, people are *fragmented.*

4. When there is no vision, people are *unproductive.*

If there is ever an accurate description of the maintenance culture life it is: unmotivated, undisciplined, fragmented, and unproductive. The maintenance culture does not give you a reason to stretch. So the enemy provides the excitement in your job, sports, and entertainment, anything but the church. The maintenance-culture church has abdicated vision, passion, and goal fulfillment to the world, but the people who live life with the greatest sense of expectancy are those living God's vision of them.

The reason you descend into the culture of maintenance is because of the absence of faith for your future. The reason there is an absence of faith is from the void of no vision in your soul—no vision, no stretching, no faith for God's grace and God's Spirit to invade our limitations with His power, no faith for God's grace to be greater than our weaknesses. When your life has descended into the maintenance culture, you need little faith for God to transform you because maintenance doesn't require change. The maintenance culture conforms you to circumstances; it says cope with life, don't conquer it. Be satisfied with mediocrity. There is no passion in the maintenance culture because there is no life-changing vision.

You will never conquer your fears of failure from the past without a greater faith for the future. Vision is the source for the greater faith required to break through. The breakthrough journey is for you to become like Jesus. The journey begins with a fresh vision because a fresh vision releases a fresh anointing.

If you are going to break through the obstacles satan has erected from past sins, mistakes, wrong decisions, and failures, you must live by vision. If you will break through the obstacles that arise before you, you must live by vision. If you will break through the barriers with which the maintenance culture oppresses your soul, you must live by vision.

Living by vision is a life skill. You cannot excuse yourself from not having vision by telling yourself, "I'm just not the kind of person who lives by vision." Living by vision is a learned skill. When you learn the skill to live by vision, you have mastered one of the most important skills to maximize your influence.

The vision life skill will release these four dynamics into your soul:

1. Vision-Motivation energizes your will with passion.

2. Vision-Focus ruthlessly eliminates distractions to achieve your goals.

3. Vision-Discipline consistently executes the plan to fulfill your mission.

4. Vision-Production maximizes every opportunity.

*Brethren, I count not myself to have apprehended: but this one thing I do, forgetting those things which are behind, and reaching forth* [I stretch] *unto those things which are before* (Philippians 3:13).

To receive one of the greatest blessings in following Jesus, you've got to stretch! To become what God created and saved you to be, you've got to stretch. To fulfill God's vision of you, you've got to stretch. I saw a great example of what it means to stretch while watching the Kansas

City Chiefs against the Dallas cow pokes. It was that crucial moment at the end of the football game when the momentum had been gained by the pokes. They had just scored. I felt the win slipping away from the Chiefs as the tension of the moment was magnified by 78,000 fans screaming for somebody to step up and be the victor.

In the huddle, Priest Holmes's number was called to run a fly pattern for a touchdown. (That means you fly down the field as fast as you can.) He is pumped as he lines up. He puts forth every ounce of energy as he flies down the field. Trent Green, the Chiefs' quarterback, throws the football so that only Priest can catch it. Priest keeps his eyes focused on the ball, but then Deion Sanders, the pokes' cornerback, bumps him, and suddenly he is off balance and off course.

He keeps his eye focused on the ball. Deion, knowing Priest is in trouble, tries to distract him by putting his hand in Priest's face. But Priest keeps his eye focused on the ball. Keeping his eye focused on the ball, Priest sees that he will not catch the ball doin' what he's doin'. It is not enough. He has got to do more. The only way to win is to stretch. Knowing he will be vulnerable to Deion's hit after he catches the ball, he leaps off the ground, extending and stretching himself out horizontally, three feet off the ground.

In this unsafe and unfamiliar situation, he keeps his eye focused on the ball, and he watches it right into his hands. At that very moment, Deion hits him with everything he's got to make him drop the ball, but Priest seized the ball and would not let it go. His body flew sideways from the hit he received, but he flew sideways across the goal line—a victor.

In that moment Priest experienced the fulfillment and joy of vision transforming losers to victors. Priest had vision-passion. He had the expectancy of being a victor because the greater one lived in his heart. He believed in his team because they all had the vision-discipline to execute the plan.

The ball was the vision. He was disciplined to execute the plan because he had to get the ball. He had to get to the vision. His passion energized his determination to invest everything to get to the vision, but at the end it took even more.

His vision-focus kept his eye on the vision. He had to keep his eyes focused on the vision the whole play. He could never lose focus of the vision, or he would lose. When you lose focus of the vision, you lose. He was focused on one thing—get to the vision. While he was running with abandonment, he kept focused on the vision. When the opposition attempted every way he could to distract him, he kept focused on the vision. When the opposition knocked him off balance, he kept focused on the vision.

When the opposition knocked him off course, he kept focused on the vision. The opposition blocked his sight, but he kept on the vision. He was focused on the vision until he seized it, and then the opposition knocked him sideways to make him drop the vision. He grasped the vision.

*You will be transformed from a victim to a victor when you live by vision.*

Priest had vision-production as he seized the opportunity to change victims into victors.

You perish without a vision because no ball is coming to you to focus on. You have no opportunity to be a victor without a vision.

When God the Father created you, He had a vision of you. He deposited gifts, talents, and abilities in you. He believes in you more than you believe in yourself because He sees you at your best. He sees your strengths at their strongest. He sees your gifts operating at their highest level. He sees your abilities fulfilled. His vision of you is an awesome vision. He knows what you can be.

He wants to throw you the ball because He cannot make you a victor without your catching the vision. The only way for you to reach God's created vision of you is for you to stretch, not thinking about the risk; rather, you stretch yourself out in abandonment of faith to fulfill His vision, and to feel His pleasure.

I asked a pastor once, "Pastor, are you stretching?" He responded, "Sure I am."

I asked, "What are you stretching toward?" He responded, "I don't know."

You can't stretch for nothing. If you don't have a vision, you cannot stretch. You cannot fulfill Philippians 3:13 without a vision for your life.

You will never feel the joy of His pleasure for fulfilling your destiny, if you do not live by vision. You will never experience the exhilaration of breaking through barriers that have been holding you down for years if you do not live by vision. You will never have an extravagant expectancy in God's multiplication without vision.

You not be able to maximize your influence, if you do not live by vision. You will either stretch toward the vision or slumber in the maintenance culture.

You will never fulfill your destiny if you do not stretch for what lies ahead. The greatest robbery the thief ever accomplishes is when he snatches the vision, faith, and passion out of your heart. Satan does not want you to stretch, nor does he want you to be motivated to abandon yourself to the ways of God. He wants you to cope and be comfortable in the maintenance culture.

Your vision is vital to your future because it is the picture of you in your future. *You cannot consistently function* in a manner that is *inconsistent* with the way you see yourself. Your picture of yourself, your vision, will determine your performance, your happiness, even the way you relate to people.

The struggle so many have is that their picture of themselves originates from the past—past experiences, things parents have said, teachers, or coaches, or friends. Often what forms our picture of ourselves are the negative things parents have said, the negative experiences, the failures, and the disappointments.

So the picture of you today is a reflection of the negative input from your past. God presents to you a big opportunity because He is a big God. You look at that big opportunity and the big challenges that accompany it. Then you tell God, "I can't do that!" The Lord says, "How do you know you can't?" And you respond, "I have never done it before." And the past controls you! The past controls your future.

God is not the great *I was.* God is the great *I AM!* He is not asking you what you have done in the past. He is asking you if you have faith in

Him to do great things in your future. You cannot have God's vision, until you have God's memory. "Your sins and your lawless deeds I will remember no more" (see Heb. 10:17). God has divine amnesia. For you to be elevated by the Spirit into your future, you must receive divine amnesia about your past. The blood of Jesus cleanses us from all sin, failure, mistakes, wrong decisions. Believe in the power of the blood.

How can you have God's vision of you and your future? You must think like God.

The Bible says that God declares the end from the beginning (see Isa. 46:10). How can God declare the end from the beginning? Because He exists outside of time.

Faith is the "evidence of things not seen" (Heb. 11:1). The only way for us to see something that is not in the natural realm is by imagination. God sees the end from the beginning, and if you are going to have God's vision of you and your future it will be by your faith-activated imagination.

The obstacle for many in the maintenance culture is they do not have a faith-activated imagination; instead they have a fear-activated imagination. Their fear gets going, and they can imagine all sorts of bad things that can happen if you stretch yourself for God. Their future is defined by their fears, so they do nothing because the picture of their future vision is painted by fear. Others have a worry-activated imagination; they just worry about all sorts of things that could go wrong. They are always asking "what if" questions. "What if this" would happen, or "what if that" would happen. After listening to the ones with a fear-activated imagination, everybody thinks it's prudent to do nothing, and they miss God.

If you are going to fulfill your destiny in God, you must think like God. You must have faith-activated imagination that sees the end—the vision of you.

A definition of vision is a picture of what God is going to be and God is going to do through me. Your vision of you, your picture of you, is no longer limited to you. Once you receive Christ, the Anointed One, living in you, God's vision can become complete. His vision of you from the foundation of the world can only be fulfilled by the life and power of the Spirit of God energizing and empowering you to stretch beyond yourself to what God will do through you.

The basis for your faith that activates your imagination is that God is empowering you to fulfill your destiny. As you release your faith to energize your imagination, you receive a vision-faith for you and your life.

Vision produces faith; faith produces passion; passion produces determination!

The purposes of God cannot be fulfilled by a passionless people. For you to have the energy to fulfill your destiny, you must have passion from your vision-faith.

**You can seize your future.**

**You can grasp your destiny.**

**You can make your way prosperous,**

**when you live by vision!**

*The just shall live by his faith* (Habakkuk 2:4).

Those whom God deems justified to receive from Him are those who live, not who are just saved, but who live, by faith. Living by faith means you must live by vision.

That revelation stirred the apostle Paul to live at a high performance and high capacity life to fulfill his destiny. Living by vision is living by faith.

*Now faith is the substance of things hoped for, the evidence of things not seen* (Hebrews 11:1).

Faith is the substance of your vision.

Faith is the evidence of your future.

The vision of your future must have the substance of faith because there will come a time of testing, the testing of your faith, when everything in the natural realm is telling you the vision will not be fulfilled, and what everyone sees is just the opposite of your vision.

People will come to you and say, "Your vision can't come about now. Look at what is happening. Do you see what is going wrong?"

At that time is when your faith will lead you to a higher level, and you will lead others to a higher level when you say, "I know my vision will be fulfilled." People will ask you, "How do you know it will be fulfilled when everything is going wrong?" You will respond, "Because I have evidence." They will say, "What is your evidence?" You will declare, "My faith is my evidence!"

In the "due season" between the sowing and the harvest of multiplication, you will need the substance of faith because the substance of circumstances will crush your vision if you do not have the substance of faith. You must have a rock-hard faith in your heart. You must have the Rock inside of you making your faith rock-hard. The enemy will crush your vision by circumstances if your vision is not built upon the Rock. You must have the substance of faith to overcome the substance of what you see.

*See the vision by faith.*

*Declare the vision by faith.*

*Walk the vision by faith.*

*Receive the vision by faith!*

*Looking unto Jesus the author and finisher of our faith; who for the joy that was set before Him endured the cross* (Hebrews 12:2).

King Jesus demonstrated living by faith, so He is the author and leader of our faith. King Jesus endured the cross; He endured the shame because of the joy set before Him. God the Father told His Son, "I have a joy for You if You will suffer on the cross. I have a reward for You if You will endure the shame of hell to destroy the power of darkness over the earth."

I have heard many sermons about going to the cross. Go to the cross, and it will make you holy. Go to the cross; it will make you righteous. But God the Father did not tell His Son to go to the cross, except for one motivation: the vision, the joy, the reward! You lead a life of vision because of the joy set before you.

> *But without faith it is impossible to please Him: for he that cometh to*
> *God must believe that He is, and that He is a rewarder of them that*
> *diligently seek Him* (Hebrews 11:6).

Many church folks read this verse, "But without faith it is hard to please God." Actually, it is *impossible* to please God without faith because you cannot fulfill His vision of your life without faith. You will not reach the heights of the ways of God without faith. You will miss the blessings of the Kingdom without faith. It is impossible to please Him because it is impossible to receive from Him without faith.

So when you come to Him you must have faith; that is an imperative necessity. There is no other way to come to God. You cannot come to Him in tears; you cannot come to Him in hope; you cannot come to Him wishing; you must come to Him in faith in order for you to receive all He has for you. You must believe He is a rewarder of them that "seek Him out." You seek Him out by faith.

I have a special relationship with my God. He is my rewarder! He has set a joy before me—the vision of what He can be and He can do through me. He wants me to come to Him for that vision-faith to be fulfilled in my life.

Faith is the substance of things hoped for. The substance of the hope of my vision is faith. Hope is defined as "optimistic expectancy of good." You cannot be a Christian and a pessimist. It is a contradiction of terms. If you are a Christian, you must be an optimist because of the joy set before you.

Here is a story to demonstrate the difference between a pessimist and an optimist. A psychologist conducted a test between a boy who was a pessimist and one who was an optimist. First, he put the pessimist in a room full of toys. A while later he returned to discover the pessimist sitting in the middle of the room with a huge pout on his face. When the psychologist asked what was wrong, the pessimistic boy replied, "There is just nothing to do!"

The psychologist then put the optimistic boy in a room with a big pile of horse manure. When he returned later, he discovered the optimistic boy in the middle of the pile, throwing manure everywhere. The psychologist rushed into the room and asked, "What are you doing?!" The optimistic boy responded, "With this much manure, there's got to be a pony somewhere!"

Some church folk talk about the pile, fellowship about the pile, pray the pile. But I've got good news for you: God's got a pony for you! If you have manure in your life, God's got a pony for you! He is your Rewarder! By His grace and power, He will fulfill His vision of you.

# 8

# YOU MAXIMIZE
# WHEN YOU MULTIPLY

Now you see the power of vision-faith in your life, so what is the vision for your life? Is it something you are to determine for yourself, or is your vision to become like Jesus—King Jesus? "To be like Jesus, to be like Jesus, all I want is to be like Him."

Here is the vision that will maximize your influence as you become a God-multiplier like the King.

*For we are His workmanship, created in Christ Jesus unto good works, which God hath before ordained that we should walk in them* (Ephesians 2:10).

The word translated "workmanship" can also be translated "masterpiece." Before the foundation of the world (see Eph. 1:4), God created you to be His Masterpiece. You are unique, special, and invaluable to God. You are God's masterpiece! If you could hear Father God speak to you right now, He would say, "You are My masterpiece. You are My unique and wonderful masterpiece of My God-creativity. I have created you to experience a maximized life by fulfilling My prepared works. I created you in My image, and I have formed you in My likeness to rule My dominion."

*And Mary said, My soul doth magnify the Lord* (Luke 1:46).

"Your soul will magnify Me when you multiply Me on earth," says almighty God.

Make this profession of faith out loud:

*I am God's masterpiece. I am uniquely created for excellent works.*

*I am a beautiful masterpiece. People see the beauty of God in Heaven through me.*

*I am a wonderful masterpiece of God-creativity.*

*I magnify on the earth when I multiply God in the souls of men.*

The Anointed One and His anointing upon me gives me the optimistic expectancy of the authority, and power, and glory of God in my life (see Col. 1:27).

You are a masterpiece when you reflect the image and rule in the likeness of God on the earth. The masterpiece is God in you. Christ in you gives the optimistic expectancy of God's presence, power, and authority

A masterpiece is a product of a "master." God does not only want you to be His masterpiece, but He also has plans for you to be a master artist magnifying His image through multiplying Him on the earth.

Genesis reveals that God created the masterpiece of man to magnify Him by multiplying His image on the earth, and there are two creative purposes ordained for you as God's masterpiece to walk in them. First, you are created in the image of God. Have you heard the expression, "He is a spittin' image of his father"? That is what God did. He created you so when people look at you they would say, "He/she is the spittin' image of their Father-God. You just can't tell them apart."

When you are in fellowship with the God in Heaven, you reflect His image on the earth. Heaven comes to earth through you. Wherever you go, people will come into contact with God through you. They will see the reflection of God in your countenance. They will see the love of God in your eyes. They will sense the presence of His Spirit when you walk in the room. God created you to be in His likeness, and they feel better about life just by being around you because they have been around God. They see the reflection of the Father in Heaven through you.

God's vision is that the masterpiece of your soul would reflect back to Him His image. When He sees His image in your soul, you magnify Him on earth, and you cause Him pleasure. It gets even better because He has ordained you to multiply His image. The good works you are to walk in is to multiply the reflection of God on the earth. The masterpiece of man is created in His image to manifest and multiply the reflection of your God in Heaven on earth.

God also said of the masterpiece of man, "Let Us make man...after Our likeness: and let them have dominion" (Gen. 1:26).

God created the masterpiece of man to manifest His dominion over the earth. God made man a living soul, not only to be in His image, but also in His likeness, demonstrating the domain of the King.

The greatest means to magnify God is to multiply His image on the earth. The greatest method to magnify God is to expand His government in Heaven to earth. God created the masterpiece of man to bring Heaven to earth. God's grand vision of the masterpiece of man was not fulfilled by the first Adam. Evil intruded on God's creative purpose for man.

*How art thou fallen from heaven, O Lucifer, son of the morning! how art thou cut down to the ground, which didst weaken the nations! For thou hast said in thine heart, I will ascend into heaven, I will exalt my throne above the stars of God: I will sit also upon the mount of the congregation, in the sides of the north: I will ascend above the heights of the clouds; I will be like the most High* (Isaiah 14:12-14).

As I read the account of how darkness entered into God's creation through the cherub, lucifer, I sensed the Lord asking me this question: What motivated lucifer to rebel against the God he was anointed to worship? Did he wake one morning in eternity past and say to himself, "I think I'll rebel against God today." Or was there an event that triggered the pride and lust for power? What made lucifer think he could be "like the most High"? When I asked His question back to Him, this is the story He uncovered in my heart.

Father God loved His Son, and as Father, He desired to give His Son an inheritance worthy of the Son of God. He created the heavens and the earth, His infinite creation, as an inheritance for the Son of God. God the Father said to the Son, "We have created man in Our image, so he will reflect the image of Our glory, and the power of Our life. He will multiply Our image and glory throughout creation. He will be like Us, ruling the domain of the King of Heaven on earth with You. The soul of man will love You, adore You, obey, and worship You as Lord and King. In the Kingdom of Heaven under Your rule, he will enjoy the abundance of My infinite creation. He will know the righteousness, peace, and joy of the Kingdom of Heaven on the earth."

Father God said, "My Son, this infinite universe is Your inheritance. I give to You to rule as only the Son of God can. You will be the King over My Kingdom on earth."

What triggered the cherub lucifer's pride and lust for power? He saw the Father give the infinite universe to His Son for His inheritance, then he said in his heart, "If I take the Son's place as lord over His inheritance of infinite creation, then I would be like God." Lucifer said, "I will exalt myself above the stars of God...I will be like the most High." Lucifer rebelled because he saw how he could be like the most High—exalt his throne above the stars of God.

He rebelled against the God he worshiped. He became the father of lies when he deceived man to follow him in rebellion. He stole the dominion over the inheritance belonging to the Son. At that moment lucifer became known throughout Heaven as "the thief" (John 10:10). He became "the god of this world" (2 Cor. 4:4).

*For, behold, the darkness shall cover the earth, and gross darkness the people: but the Lord shall arise upon thee, and His glory shall be seen upon thee* (Isaiah 60:2).

Not only did satan steal the Son's inheritance, he also stole the vision of the masterpiece of man multiplying God's image and in the likeness of God ruling the dominion of Heaven. He knew that if the soul of man would ever again be God's masterpiece that his power of darkness would be broken. Deep darkness blinded the eyes of man from seeing himself as the masterpiece God created him to be. Fearing man's potential to be like God, satan bound him in darkness. Deprived of God's vision, the soul of man became like the creatures, and not like the Creator.

Instead of a living soul reflecting the image of God, man became oppressed by fear, weakened by hopelessness, and burdened with guilt.

Beaten down into subjection to the forces of evil, the damaged and disabled soul of man no longer had the capacity to reflect His glory or the strength to exert His heavenly authority.

In this deficient state, satan stole his abundance, and man lived in poverty; he stole his health, and man lived in the distress of a diseased body and died; and satan stole his joy, the bruised soul was afflicted with a spirit of heaviness. Instead of a victor, man became a victim; instead of a conqueror, man, created in the image of the Creator, became conquered.

Polluted hearts and defective souls could not withstand the curse from the unrelenting attacks of the evil darkness. God's masterpiece vision, the living soul of man, became a deficient and disabled soul. In the deep darkness of satan's power, the soul of man became a victim of darkness.

*Who hath delivered us from the power of darkness, and hath translated us into the kingdom of His dear Son* (Colossians 1:13).

At the fullness of time, God the Father turned to His Son-King and said, "Son, it is time to establish the Kingdom of Heaven on the earth and take back Your inheritance by restoring the soul of man to be in Our image, after Our likeness."

*And He said unto them, I must preach the kingdom of God to other cities also: for therefore am I sent* (Luke 4:43).

The Father thrust His Son to earth with one mission mandate: **Establish the Kingdom.** The mission mandate required an indisputable proactive strategy: **Invade darkness.**

King Jesus' invasive mission to plunder the domain of darkness began the Great War in the unseen spiritual realm between the Kingdom of Heaven and the kingdom of darkness.

**King Jesus did not invade darkness to save mankind;**

**King Jesus saved mankind to invade darkness.**

King Jesus did not invade darkness to save mankind; He invaded darkness to multiply the image of God on the earth to establish the Kingdom so the will of God would overrule the schemes of satan.

*When a strong man armed keepeth his palace, his goods are in peace: but when a stronger than he [King Jesus] shall come upon him [invade], and overcome him, he taketh from him all his armour wherein he trusted, and divideth his spoils* (Luke 11:21-22).

Jesus outlined the Kingdom strategy: Invade darkness; conquer the forces of evil; plunder their armor (see Ezek. 30:22); render them defenseless against the Kingdom of Heaven; and lead victims of darkness into His Kingdom.

### Jesus was an invasive King.

### Jesus was an interruptive King.

### Jesus was an intrusive King.

King Jesus invaded darkness to restore God's masterpiece vision for the soul of man to reflect His image and expand His Kingdom. Victims oppressed by the power of darkness will be translated into His Kingdom transformed from the deficient soul to a prosperous soul (see 3 John 2). The prosperous soul of the new Kingdom once again has the capacity to reflect the image of God, multiply the image of God, and expand the authority of God. The creative purpose of man would be fulfilled in the Kingdom of Heaven.

Jesus was sent from Heaven to multiply God on the earth. His message was, "Repent, for the kingdom of heaven is at hand" (Matt. 3:2 NKJV). Jesus declared that a new Kingdom had come upon the earth. "You don't have to be oppressed. You don't have to be defeated. You don't have to be blinded. You don't have to be poor. You don't have to be tormented. Get out of darkness, and get into the Kingdom of Heaven!"

Getting into the Kingdom of Heaven came by God's getting in you!

*Jesus answered and said unto him, Verily, verily, I say unto thee, Except a man be born again, he cannot see the kingdom of God* (John 3:3).

This transformation of the deficient, disabled, and darkened soul of man to his original creative purpose—to once again reflect the beauty of God on earth—can only be accomplished by a heavenly birth. Heaven will open so the Spirit of God will fill the soul of man once again. Entrance into this alternative God Kingdom is by the God Spirit making the God Image in the soul of man. Jesus is the first God-multiplier!

## JESUS IS HEAVEN'S GOD-MULTIPLIER

Multiplying God on the earth created a new Kingdom-culture of faith instead of fear; a culture of freedom instead of oppression; a culture of prosperity instead of poverty; a culture of strength instead of weakness; and a culture of health instead of sickness.

The Kingdom of Heaven is a new way of living. It is the culture of victors. In this Kingdom-culture the mission of King Jesus to multiply God's image would be the mission of man to be fruitful and multiply in the Kingdom. Man would once again be the God-multiplier! Man would once again, after God's likeness, exert His rule over the earth.

The Kingdom-culture changed those led out of darkness because they no longer saw themselves oppressed, poor, and weak. They no longer saw their soul always harassed by the devil, telling anyone who would listen, "The devil has been after me." They saw God's vision of a prosperous soul: reflecting His image, and ruling like Him. In the Kingdom-culture, victims became strong, conquering, ruling, and passionate. Their eyes were opened to see satan, the disarmed and defeated oppressor who must bow at the name of their new King—Jesus! The Kingdom-church has the Kingdom-culture.

*The Kingdom-culture is what transforms church members into God-multipliers.*

What satan feared came upon him. God's original vision was fulfilled of the masterpiece of man becoming the God-multiplier, expanding the God Kingdom, bringing Heaven to earth.

## THE PROSPEROUS SOUL OF THE KINGDOM

Repenting, turning away from darkness toward Heaven to believe in the gospel of the Kingdom of Heaven, makes your polluted heart, your disabled soul, have the capability to receive the Spirit coming out of

Heaven. You are born again from above. The Spirit has come upon you to give you the capacity to reflect God through your soul.

The Kingdom of Heaven fulfills the creative vision of God. In the beginning man became a living soul. In the Kingdom man became a prosperous soul.

*Beloved, I wish above all things that thou mayest prosper and be in health, even as thy soul prospereth* (3 John 2).

An increasingly prosperous soul continuously maximizes your capability to live at a high capacity and high performance life through exerting Kingdom authority and anointing.

Kingdom-culture will maximize your influence. The maintenance culture marginalizes your influence. The Kingdom-culture will maximize your influence to experience the maximum potential of the masterpiece of man. The Kingdom-culture enlarges your capacity to receive from Heaven and release Heaven on the earth.

## The Church's Mission Has the Kingdom Strategy

Jesus invaded darkness to take back His inheritance. He declares His church has the same mission strategy.

• *Jesus **invaded** the kingdom of darkness.*

• *Jesus **conquered** the forces of darkness.*

• *Jesus **plundered** the victims of darkness.*

• *Jesus **ruled** over the expanding Kingdom of Heaven on the earth.*

King Jesus' command to the church was: Rule in the midst of your enemies!

*Or else how can one enter into a strong man's house, and spoil his goods, except he first bind the strong man? and then he will spoil his house* (Matthew 12:29).

His Lordship over dark forces would not be demonstrated only through Him, but through the victims satan had tormented, damaged, and disabled.

The oppressed now became the oppressors.

The conquered now became the conquerors.

The poor plundered the palace goods.

God-multipliers do not allow the devil to set the agenda for their lives by being reactive, defeated victims hiding in church. God-multipliers set the agenda by invading satan's kingdom to plunder his palace and take possession of their inheritance. God-multipliers don't confess that "the devil is after me." God-multipliers confess, "I am after the devil!" In this new Kingdom-culture, passion to plunder darkness burns in their hearts.

The Father's mandate to establish a counter-culture Kingdom required the victims of the kingdom of darkness to follow Kingdom strategy: Invade darkness, conquer evil forces, plunder their palace, and multiply God on the earth.

When victims became God-multipliers exerting Kingdom authority over evil forces to plunder satan's goods, the masterpiece vision of man was complete. Man magnified God's authority, and only then was satan's power of darkness broken over the earth.

*And the seventy returned again with joy, saying, Lord, even the devils are subject unto us through Thy name. And He said unto them, I beheld Satan as lightning fall from heaven* (Luke 10:17-18).

King Jesus equipped the God-multipliers with the armor of light (see Rom. 13:4; Eph. 6:10-17) causing the forces of darkness to flee in terror from those they once oppressed. Evil forces cannot prevail against the sword of the Spirit set on fire by the passionate faith declared out of the mouth of the God-multipliers in the new Kingdom.

## KINGS IN THE KINGDOM

*And He hath on His vesture and on His thigh a name written, KING OF KINGS, AND LORD OF LORDS* (Revelation 19:16).

*He that overcometh* [conquers] *shall inherit all things; and I will be his God, and he shall be My son. But the fearful, and unbelieving...* (Revelation 21:7-8).

The word *overcometh* should be translated "conquers." It means "to carry off the victory." A conqueror carries off the victory spoils. In the reactive maintenance culture, overcoming means, "Satan came to me to tempt me, but I overcame his temptation."

In the Kingdom of Heaven, conquering satan doesn't mean that I withstood satan. It means that satan could not withstand me. I invaded and conquered him. Often, in Revelation it says "conquers" instead of "overcometh," and it provides a more accurate picture of the heart attitude and behavior Father God is searching for in the Kingdom.

The heart of a conqueror reflects the image of King Jesus who conquered the world (see John 16:33). Conquering and plundering darkness is your created destiny: Be like Jesus, a God-multiplier! Jesus tells a parable about multipliers who are rewarded by being rulers over the domain of cities (see Luke 19:17). Multiplication is rewarded by King Jesus. Multipliers will be rulers in the coming age. Ruling over a domain of cities is the position of a king. God-multipliers will be rewarded to be kings with the King.

God's vision from the foundations of the world was for His masterpiece creation man to rule as king. The qualification to fulfill God's vision of you to reign as king with King Jesus is for you to be a God-multiplier like King Jesus.

God's eternal vision of man to reflect His Image and rule in His Kingdom will be fulfilled when the King returns. Jesus, as the King of kings and the Lord of lords, will return, leading the *armies* out of Heaven (see Rev. 19:14-16). There is not just one army following one king. There are armies out of Heaven following many kings. The King who conquered hell and plundered hell will lead the kings who conquered darkness. The King and his kings will smite the nations and rule over them.

**Your redeemed destiny awaits your invasion.**

*To be a Ruler, you must be a Multiplier.*

*To be a Multiplier, you must be a Plunderer.*

*To be a Plunderer, you must be a Conqueror.*

*To be a Conqueror, you must be an Invader.*

Jesus invaded darkness to establish an ever-expanding, counter-culture Kingdom of Heaven on the earth (see Luke 4:43). When disciples are no longer made, darkness is no longer invaded, and the Kingdom is not expanded. The only culture that cannot become infected with the maintenance culture is the Kingdom-church culture.

# 9

# MAXIMIZE THE FATHER'S BUSINESS

You have a big God! Your big God has a big vision for you to do something big in your big church! He has big plans for His Church to expand the Kingdom of Heaven on the earth, pushing back the forces of darkness, to lead those captive by darkness to freedom. You are a big part of His Kingdom expansion plans! God has plans for ordinary Christians, just like you, to do extraordinary exploits in His Kingdom. These are the greatest days the church of King Jesus will ever experience. You do not want to be on the sidelines, missing your destiny, when hurting humanity turns to King Jesus and His church rises up in power and might.

> *And He said unto them, When ye pray, say, Our Father which art in heaven, hallowed be Thy name. Thy kingdom come* [out of heaven to earth]. *Thy will be done, as in heaven, so in earth* (Luke 11:2).

When Jesus taught us to pray, He did not teach us to pray for the church to grow, or for the church to be better at teaching the members. He did not teach us to pray for the 47 to 125 wonderful programs your church may offer. Jesus taught us to pray that the Kingdom—the authority and dominion of God—would expand on the earth just as it is in Heaven. King Jesus' church worldview did not originate with people and the church on earth, but God and His Kingdom in Heaven coming to earth.

In the Gospels, the Kingdom is mentioned 124 times, the church is referred to only twice. King Jesus declared His purpose for being sent from Heaven was to proclaim and establish the Kingdom of Heaven on earth.

*And He* [Jesus] *said unto them, I must preach the kingdom of God to other cities also: for therefore am I sent* (Luke 4:43).

God the Father did not send His Son to proclaim the church. He sent His son to proclaim and establish the Kingdom of Heaven upon the earth.

Jesus' message was not about the church, but about the Kingdom.

*From that time Jesus began to preach, and to say, Repent: for the kingdom of heaven is at hand.... And Jesus went about all Galilee, teaching in their synagogues, and preaching the gospel of the kingdom, and healing all manner of sickness and all manner of disease among the people* (Matthew 4:17,23).

The Book of Acts—the book telling of the story of the early Church—began with the Kingdom, ended with the Kingdom, and proclaimed the Kingdom.

The Book of Acts begins with the Kingdom:

*To whom* [His apostles] *also He showed Himself alive after His passion by many infallible proofs, being seen of them forty days, and* **speaking of the things pertaining to the kingdom of God** (Acts 1:3).

The Book of Acts ends in the very last chapter in the very last verse with the apostle Paul preaching the Kingdom:

**Preaching the kingdom of God,** *and teaching those things which concern the Lord Jesus Christ, with all confidence, no man forbidding him* (Acts 28:31).

The message of Acts was the same message that King Jesus preached:

*But when they believed Philip preaching the things concerning the kingdom of God, and the name of Jesus Christ, they were baptized, both men and women* (Acts 8:12).

---

The good news that sinners believed was not about joining a wonderful church, but sinners heard about the Kingdom of Heaven. Then they changed—not from a mean person who smoked and drank to nice person who went to meetings on Sunday. They changed kingdoms. The Acts church turned the world upside down by proclaiming the Kingdom of Heaven, leading victims of darkness out of the power of darkness and translating them into the Kingdom of Heaven.

The Acts church was the Kingdom-church with the same mission of King Jesus: Establish the ever-expanding Kingdom of God on the earth. Every disciple was engaged in Kingdom expansion in their kingdom-realm.

How are you going to see your church the way God sees His church? By faith!

The Bible says you either live by faith or by sight (see 2 Cor. 5:7). God's big plans are only available to you when you walk by faith. It is impossible to please God when you live by sight because you limit God to what you can see (see Heb. 11:6). He loves you too much and wants to prosper you beyond the limitations of your sight.

As you see how big your Kingdom-church is, some good church members may not like seeing that big church. Sometimes they don't want to be part of a growing church that is getting bigger. For those good people who want to remain in the comfort zone of a small, slow-growing church, sometimes the best thing for them is to go to a church that doesn't have a vision of the Kingdom-church. There are lots of churches that have a small vision of their church.

When they do leave, don't be like some church members who allow their fear or activated imagination tell them that if they lose people then the church will get smaller—which makes the mission of the church become simply to keep all the folks in the building. Fear-activated imagination says: *If we lose people, the church will get smaller.*

Those church folks are like a football team that has a one-point lead and thinks that if they can just maintain that one-point lead, then they will win the game. They are afraid that if they lose that one point they will lose the game. The team plays not to win but instead plays not to lose, but when you play not to lose, you will lose.

The Kingdom-church vision sees the church not defined by buildings, but by relationships. The Kingdom-church vision is big and ever-expanding, just like the Kingdom. The Kingdom-church vision creates an expectancy in the hearts of disciples of King Jesus and invites God to do something big!

## THE MAINTENANCE-CULTURE VISION: BUILDING CHURCH

The maintenance-culture values define the church as those who attend the meetings in the building. The Building Church vision limits the church to those you see attending the meetings in the building. This vision is walking by sight.

The Building Church ministry is primarily to church members in the building, so the majority of the ministry and the "important" ministry occurs in the building. Even the churches that have small groups outside of the church building can have the Building Church vision because the small groups are provided for the church members of the building. This vision does not motivate the church to meet needs of anyone other than those in the building.

The Building Church vision limits God to what we can see—a church building. God does not want to be limited to your church building because there are more needs outside of the building than inside of the building. There are more miracles outside of the church building than inside the church building.

## Maintenance-Culture Vision: Building Church

BUILDING CHURCH

STAFF

Building Church
- People who come to the building
- In the model, the staff ministers.
- Ministry occurs primarily in the building.
- Limited view of church

The Building Church vision has produced a ministry model of lack, limitations, and loneliness. It has two fundamental components: the professional caregivers, and the church members who hire them to receive their care. When more caregiving is needed, the solution is to hire more staff. Those with the Building Church vision think that the church exists primarily to nurture and maintain the church members.

The limitation of the Building Church vision is that the church budget cannot afford to hire enough professionals to care for all the church members. Professional caregivers cannot meet the heart-felt needs of church members, and often the pews are filled with lonely people. People do not have the relational support to live out their vision.

There are too many needs, and the staff gets worn out from caregiving. They do not have the energy to produce training materials to empower members to live at a higher level. The best the caregiving staff can do is maintain the Building Church.

It is impossible for God's plans for you—big plans—to be fulfilled in His big Kingdom-church by this vision and mission. God is a big God.

This vision concludes that the church members are the responsibility of the church leadership and staff. In this model, the staff are the caregivers and the members are the recipients of whatever ministry is provided.

The Building Church vision defines the ministry to nurture and maintain the church members in the building. While the Building Church vision may state that the church is there to meet the needs of the community, the primary needs it is focused on are those in the building. This vision cannot see beyond the building, nor beyond the church members, for a bigger picture and purpose of the church.

The faith that God is a big God and has big plans for you in His Big Church cannot survive in the Building Church vision. God's mission for your life is greater than what can happen in the Building Church vision.

## THE KINGDOM-CHURCH VISION

The Kingdom-church vision is Jesus' big vision of His Church because it expresses the Father's heart of faith and love. The Kingdom-church vision has biblical principles restoring biblical power.

The biblical Church was not defined by meetings, but by relationships. Paul tells us we are "members one of another" (Rom. 12:5), not members of an institution. The Kingdom-church vision captures the mission of the church because this vision does not define the church by meetings in a building, but by relationships of the heart. This vision increases your faith as you see His Kingdom-church beyond the church building.

Before the foundation of the world (see Eph. 1:4), God chose you to be part of His big vision of His Church. In the same way, God has already chosen those unchurched and unsaved in your kingdom-realm in Jesus Christ as part of your church before the foundation of the world (see Eph. 1:4).

Because the Father has chosen them from the foundation of the world, He knows the name, address, phone number, and E-mail address of every person He has chosen to be part of your Kingdom-church. They are members of your church as much as the folks who have been there for 20 years. They are your members, not Building Church members, but Kingdom-church members.

God already sees them as part of your church. Before these unchurched and unsaved people ever darken the doorstep of your church building, God sees them as members of the Kingdom-church. How can God see them as part of your Kingdom-church when they don't even know your church's address? By faith—the same way He wants you to look at your Kingdom-church.

God sees your church bigger than just the Church Building members. God sees by faith the members of your Kingdom-church, and includes them in your ministry because they are part of His big vision of your Kingdom-church. These members don't know the Father's love yet because our Building Church members, who have relationships with them, have not demonstrated the Father's love for them.

The Kingdom-church members don't call you to tell you their problems. They don't call you to tell you they are in the hospital. You will never know their needs until you become their neighbor (see Luke 10:27-37).

# The Kingdom-Church

- 75% - 96% attend because invited
- 75% want relationships
- 20 friends in your kingdom-realm
- Your church ministry is not to the "Building Church"—but to the Kingdom-church

God's bigger vision stretches your vision of your church bigger, and also stretches your vision of you bigger. Your ministry and mission is bigger. The big God in you is going to do something big through you! Because God has a big vision of you doing something big in His big Kingdom-church, you can no longer be just the recipients of the ministry. That is too small for the big God in you.

## YOUR KINGDOM-REALM

You will maximize your influence in your Kingdom-church when you see your kingdom-realm and identify those whom the Lord has already prepared for you to minister to. When you have a vision of the Kingdom-church, then your ministry becomes so much larger than what can happen in the church building.

*But we will not boast of things without our measure, but according to the measure of the rule* [or realm] *which God hath distributed to us, a measure to reach even unto you* (2 Corinthians 10:13).

You have a realm of Kingdom influence. God has distributed to you a measure of the Kingdom-church; it is your kingdom-realm to invade with Kingdom authority and the love of God to plunder and deliver victims of darkness into the Kingdom of Heaven on the earth.

What defines the reach of your kingdom-realm? Your realm is defined by your relationships with those who are held captive in the kingdom of darkness. Your reach is limited only by your willingness to love those wounded from the darkness in this world. Most Christians know 20 people who are either de-churched or unsaved. Neither is under the covering and blessing of God's Kingdom in His Church. The de-churched are attempting to fight this war by themselves, without the covering of a pastor. The unsaved do not know the blessings of peace, security, and rest found in the Kingdom-church.

Your greatest and most exciting ministry is not in a Sunday school classroom, or in a church program, but in your kingdom-realm.

## YOU WILL MINISTER TO THE MULTITUDES

*But when He saw the multitudes, He was moved with compassion on them, because they fainted, and were scattered abroad, as sheep having no shepherd* (Matthew 9:36).

"But when He saw the multitudes...." Seeing the multitudes is having the eyes of faith to see beyond the church building to see miracles disguised as needs. Every victim of darkness in your realm is a miracle waiting for you to see them with the eyes of faith.

They are fainting because satan has overcome them with discouragement and despair. They have no spiritual covering of the pastor and the church to protect them from the onslaught of the forces of darkness. They are scattered, wandering, with no clear direction, no true north in their spirit, yearning for the significance of their destiny, unable to go beyond the superficial existence consuming their time and life with things that do not fulfill the hunger in the soul of man without God. They attempt to find peace where there is no peace.

Jesus commanded us, "Lift up your eyes, and look..." (John 4:35). We must see those "multitudes" in our kingdom-realm with eyes of compassion from the Father's heart. Father God desires you to see that the vision of your mission is bigger than the church programs in the church building. See the multitudes fainting in your kingdom-realm.

Lift up your eyes; see the church bigger. See God bigger. See your mission bigger. Lift up your eyes and become part of God's big plans for His big Church.

## RELATIONAL DYNAMICS

Relationships release the love of God. The Kingdom of Heaven is expanded upon the earth when victims of darkness experience the liberating love of God through the love of a follower of the Anointed King.

The love of God poured out in your heart (see Rom. 5:5) is to be poured out upon those unchurched and unsaved in your realm of influence—your kingdom-realm. You maximize your influence by identifying those relational connections, then identifying those whom the Spirit of the Lord has made receptive to the Kingdom. Your kingdom-realm is the measure God has given to you to expand the Kingdom of Heaven, plundering your inheritance from the forces of darkness.

The relationships you have with unchurched and unsaved connect them to the Kingdom-church. Most church members know 20 people on a first-name basis who are either unchurched or unsaved. You may not be friends with these unchurched and unsaved people, but you know them on a first-name basis. Your relationship is God's opportunity for you to show the love of God to them, then lead them by love into the Fellowship of the Kingdom.

Who are these 20 first-name unsaved or unchurched friends? The hairdresser; the barber; the neighbors; the work associates; the parents of the children's team members on the baseball team, soccer team, or basketball team; the in-laws and outlaws; the people at the grocery store or convenience store. Why don't you stop right now and make a list of all the people you know who are in the kingdom-realm of your influence?

- Research has found that 75-96 percent of the visitors who attend a church are there because a church member invited them. A church member had the compassion and faith to invite a friend to church. The unchurched/unsaved person was motivated by love to attend.

- Unchurched and unsaved people want someone to invite them to church. Fully 25 percent of unchurched Americans indicate they would attend if someone would just invite them. If you invite four people to church, usually at least one will attend church with you.

In one of my pastorates, a leader of one of our small groups divorced his wife and dropped out of church for several years. Because he destroyed two families by his actions, he had a tremendous weight of guilt that kept him away from church. His journey back was through watching church on TV. He then was invited to a church, which he attended one time. He felt unworthy of attending church; he was afraid that if they knew he divorced his wife they would not want him around, so he did not return. This church continued to call him every month for six months. After the sixth call he told me, "Ken, I guess they must have wanted me because they kept calling." He now attends a church with which he disagrees theologically, but because of the persistence of their love he is now in a restored relationship with the Lord.

Church members are too afraid of offending people by "bothering them," when the real fear should be that we have not demonstrated love consistently enough for the person to believe we really do care about them, and we really do want them to go to church with us.

- The relationship with a member who invites their friends to attend church motivates visitors to attend a strange church, with strange worship, and strange people.

- Seventy-five percent of the visitors who attend your church are looking for a relationship.

Visitors attend your church needing relationships—friends. They are looking for someone to care for them, love them, and make them feel important. People come to your church looking for someone to love them and help them feel like they belong to your church.

Visitors become part of the core of your church because of relationships with someone inside the core. They cannot become part of the core through tasks or committees, but through relationships. The core of the church is comprised of people who love each other. Therefore, the only way someone can become part of the core is for someone in the core to love them into the core through relationships.

The entire process of making a disciple in the Kingdom-church is motivated by the love of God given through a relationship. Your church is transformed into the Kingdom-church when church members recognize the receptive damaged and disabled souls in their kingdom-realm, then invade with God's love to lead them into the Kingdom. Buildings have never made a disciple for Jesus Christ; only people having loving relationships can make disciples.

God sees your church as big as your Kingdom-church. Your church is as big as the total number of unchurched and unsaved people known on a first-name basis by the people attending your church. Complete this simple equation to see your church as big as your big God sees your church:

| | |
|---|---|
| Current total weekend attendance | _____ |
| Unsaved/churched in members' kingdom-realm | X 20 |
| | |
| God sees your Kingdom-church this big! | = _____ |

If your church attendance is 100, God sees your Kingdom-church as 2,000 members!

If your church attendance is 400, God sees your Kingdom-church as 8,000 members!

If your church attendance is 1,000, God sees your Kingdom-church as 20,000 members!

If your church attendance is 5,000, God sees your Kingdom-church as 100,000 members!

If your church attendance is 25,000, God sees your Kingdom-church as 500,000 members!

## KINGDOM-CHURCH MEMBERS!

If your attendance in the Building Church is 100, the Lord sees your Kingdom-church as 2,000 people. You have 1,900 folks to be led into the Kingdom.

If you are a church of 400, the Lord sees your Kingdom-church as 8,000 people. You have 7,600 members who haven't received the Lord—yet.

If you are a church of 1,000, the Lord sees your Kingdom-church as 20,000. You have 19,000 members who haven't received the Lord—yet.

If you are a church of 5,000, the Lord sees your Kingdom-church as 100,000. You have 95,000 members who haven't received the Lord—yet.

Many of you are asking me, "How can you say that God sees my church 20 times bigger than what it is?" Because God is the shepherd not just of the gathered, but of the scattered:

*As a shepherd **seeketh out his flock** in the day that he is among his sheep that are scattered; so will I seek out My sheep, and will deliver them out of all places where they have been scattered in the cloudy and dark day* (Ezekiel 34:12).

"As a shepherd seeks out his flock in the day he stands among his scattered sheep." The Building Church is the gathered flock. The Kingdom-church is the scattered flock. The Lord is standing among the scattered flock of your Kingdom-church to seek out those whose hearts are ready to receive His love and His mercy.

"His flock" are the scattered, not just the gathered. The Kingdom-church is God's church because it an inclusive vision. The Kingdom-church includes the scattered flock.

"God's sheep" are not just those gathered in the building. God's sheep are the scattered victims of darkness in the kingdom-realms of every church member in your church.

The scattered flock is the part of your church that, through relationships, are now within your church's circle of influence. There are people already prepared for divine appointments with your members to be shown the love of God.

You see, God's vision of your church is greater than the building because His compassion is greater. God doesn't just stand among the gathered (where two or more are gathered is our mentality). No, God doesn't stand just among the gathered; God stands among the scattered.

When He stands among the scattered, He sees their pain, discouragement, and wounds. He sees the lives that are being wasted on nothing, people without hope, because they do not have God's created vision for them. He sees people wanting passion, but who do not have the purposes of God; people searching for significance, but they do not have the Father's mission of life; people wanting direction for their lives, but they are missing the true north of Jesus Christ; people needing strength, but they do not know the Spirit of God. He sees the lives that are oppressed by the devil and his deceptive demons. And God says, "I will shepherd My flock."

If you want the vision of God—the big vision that God has of your church—you must also have the compassion that God has for His scattered sheep. If you desire to have the heart of God for your church, you must have the vision of God of your church. God wants you not to stand just among the gathered, but He wants you to stand among the scattered.

Those who have been part of your church from the foundation of the world, they have yet to darken the doors of your church building, but they are part of your church just as much as the sister who has faithfully attended Sunday school for 20 years.

God is calling you now, "Stand with Me among My scattered sheep. Seek out the scattered sheep of your church with My Spirit. Seek out the scattered who do not know My forgiveness, do not know My healing, do not know My love. Stand with Me and seek out the scattered sheep. Stand with Me among the scattered sheep."

*What man of you, having an hundred sheep, if he lose one of them, doth not leave the ninety and nine in the wilderness, and go after that which is lost, until he find it? ...I say unto you, that likewise joy shall be in heaven over one sinner that repenteth, more than over ninety and nine just persons, which need no repentance (Luke 15:4,7).*

Jesus saw the scattered multitudes needing the Father's compassion. God saw the scattered sheep of Israel and stood in the midst of the scattered. Jesus commands us to leave the 99 who need no repentance, and seek the wounded ones whose repentance will bring them into the Kingdom of Heaven.

The vision of the Kingdom-church multiplies ministry opportunity. The vision of the kingdom-realm leads church members out of buildings to possess their inheritance stolen by the forces of darkness. The kingdom-realm of each disciple of the Anointed King transforms the mission of the staff from nurturing and maintaining the Building Church members, to equipping and empowering church members to invade their kingdom-realm with the love and Spirit of God.

The Building Church vision produces lack, limitations, and barrenness because it does not have the eyes of faith to see the divine appointments God gives each church member in their kingdom-realm. They do not have eyes to see; they miss their mission of life the Lord has for them. They miss being the miraculous divine appointment that the Lord has prepared for them in the measure the Lord has distributed to them. They miss the joy of salvation, and they miss becoming more like Jesus. They miss their mission because they do not have eyes to see, nor ears to hear.

When your vision of your church is the Building Church, you are asking the wrong set of questions. The only questions you are asking are questions about how to care for the Building Church members. God's vision and power is greater than taking care of the church members.

He wants you to ask a different set of questions. When you begin to ask the questions God wants to answer, then you will begin to receive a spirit of wisdom and revelation from Him.

Church members may complain, "We can't even care for the folks who attend the services, much less hundreds and thousands of people in the Kingdom-church." However, God is a big God, and that big God lives in you! He is the one who will meet people at their point of need. He is the one who will increase your faith.

He is the one will be a miracle through you. When you say yes to His vision beyond the Building Church, when you say yes to His mission beyond the maintenance of members, then you can become part of God's big plans for His Church, and His big plans become part of your life.

Once you see that your ministry is for the scattered sheep in your Kingdom-church, then you will begin to ask the right questions. When you begin to ask Him how to care for the Kingdom-church, then you will be asking Him the questions He has been wanting to answer for a long time.

Let me give you an example. I am sure you have conducted a marriage seminar for your church members, so we will use that as our illustration.

Strong families make strong churches, so when we invest in marriages we are making the church stronger. We calculate that if 80 to 100 people attend the marriage seminar (in a church of 400), we would consider it a successful seminar. So the prayer team prays for 80 to 100 members to sign up for the marriage seminar. There is one specific family that is on the prayer list—it's the family whose kids are causing trouble in our children's church. If that family will attend, and the parents provide a better home for their children, that will solve the problem in our children's church!

Praise God, we have a wonderful marriage seminar! Around 80 people attend, and the family with the misbehaving child does too. We think we had a wonderful marriage seminar.

Church, what would happen if the big God in you did something big? Why not invite all the members of your church to the marriage seminar? Invite your Kingdom-church to the seminar. Why? Because the needs of the Kingdom-church mirror—are the same as—your Building Church. A church whose attendance is 400 has 8,000 in its Kingdom-church. How many of those 8,000 have marital problems? Pretty much all of them!

What would happen if instead of only inviting the 400 in the Building Church to attend the marriage seminar, you invited 8,000 members of your Kingdom-church to attend? The Kingdom of Heaven would come into their lives. People would receive the Lord, families would be restored, lives would be changed, and children would get their parents back! Why? Because your big God put a big mission in front of you and He is wanting something big through you!

## THE WOUNDED AT THEIR CHANGE POINTS

The Lord arranges seasons in the lives of the victims of darkness when they feel off-balance through difficult circumstances, which become change points as they look for answers beyond themselves. They are looking for Jesus the Anointed One to invade their lives and deliver them from the mess they are in.

Change points are personal stressful events: divorce, death in the family, lost job, financial stress, promotion, demotion, marriage, birth of a child, move, etc. These events create a need for someone beyond themselves for help. How many people in your kingdom-realm are at a change point looking for Jesus to help them through the stress of life? Approximately 10 percent.

Let me give you an example from my life. I was trying out a new hairdresser for the second time, when another hairdresser approached her, and asked, "Will you be here tomorrow at noon?" Laura, my hairdresser, was unsure and responded, "I am working a half day tomorrow, so I don't know. Why?"

The other woman excitedly said, "*He* will be here tomorrow at noon." I saw in the look on Laura's face that she was not interested in whoever he was, so after the other hairdresser left I asked, "What was that about?" Laura explained, "I had a divorce a year ago, and now people are trying to fix me up with guys, but I am just not ready."

[The Maximize Your World training will identify the people in your kingdom-realm who have been prepared by the Lord to receive the good news from you. See author's page for contact information to obtain additional training material.]

Laura is a stranger to me. I know her on a first-name basis, but she is going through a change point, off-balanced, and open to change and open to Jesus Christ if approached the proper way and with much prayer.

Now was it an accident that I was in the chair at the moment the other woman chose to approach Laura about this wonderful opportunity? Was it an accident that I discovered she is still in the midst of one of the two strongest change points in a person's life? Or was it a divine appointment for me to begin praying for her and sharing with her how Jesus heals the brokenhearted?

So many times the Spirit of God arranges divine appointments in our lives to share the love and good news in Jesus Christ, but we are not lifting up our eyes, we are not looking at opportunities, and the miracle God has for us—the miracle of loving the wounded—is missed. How many times have church members missed God because they did not see their relationships with the unchurched and unsaved as part of their church?

Each one of your church members not only know 20 people who are unchurched or unsaved, but 10 percent of them are at a change point and ready to receive Jesus Christ.

In a church of 100, a Kingdom-church of 2,000—*200 hurting people will say yes to King Jesus.*

In a church of 400, a Kingdom-church of 8,000—*800 will say yes to King Jesus!*

In a church of 1,000, a Kingdom-church of 20,000—*2,000 are ready to receive Jesus!*

In a church of 5,000, a Kingdom-church of 100,000—*10,000 are ready to receive Jesus!*

If your Building Church is a church of 400, God sees your Kingdom-church as 8,000, and it just so happens that 7,600 are not saved yet!

How many people are in a change point in your Kingdom-church? Go ahead and do the math:

| | |
|---|---|
| Kingdom-church attendance | _____ |
| Change-point percentage | X .10 |
| People ready to receive Jesus right now | = _____ |

Right now your church knows hundreds and thousands of people who are ready to receive the Lord, ready for change, needing God. The problem is that we do not have eyes to see them because our church members neither see them as part of their church, nor part of their realm. When the church becomes the Kingdom-church, and our members see their kingdom-realm, that vision will lead us out of the building into the measure the Lord has distributed to each church member.

These yet-to-be-saved members are people in the kingdom-realm of your church members, but the church members do not feel responsible to reach out because those people are not part of "my church." These people include:

— The guy at work going through a divorce. "He isn't my responsibility because he is a work associate; he is not part of my church." But he is part of your kingdom-realm.

— The woman at work who complains about her kids being out of control. "She is not my responsibility. I think she's Catholic anyway; she wouldn't be interested."

— Your hairdresser, complaining about her husband.

— The relative who has lost his job.

Once church members begin to see the church the way the Lord sees the church—the Kingdom-church—then they will see the divine appointments the Lord has distributed to them; then they will see the miracles the Lord has for them; then they will have a heart of compassion to move them to meet people at their point of need.

The kingdom-realm is given to us by the Lord to do something big for Him. Our personal kingdom-realm consists of people who know us, have a relationship with us, and need our compassion. The Lord has placed them in our kingdom-realm to demonstrate His love for them and declare His good news to them.

When you catch the vision that there is a big God in you and He has big plans for you in His big Church, then you will become a big miracle in someone's life. When you have eyes of compassion to see the wounded, fainting, and damaged in your kingdom-realm, you will be the miracle God saved you to be.

> *The Building Church vision will never release the big God in you.*
>
> *The Kingdom-church will give you a big vision of God's big church to do something big for Him!*

## BE A GOD-MULTIPLIER IN YOUR KINGDOM-REALM

Act out the vision of you being like King Jesus. Invade your kingdom-realm with the love and power of the Spirit of God! You will demonstrate that the dominion of God comes to earth through ordinary Christians who believe they have an extraordinary God. Your love will invade darkness to heal the damaged soul of a victim of the enemy and transform them into a victor! The big vision the Lord has of you will be fulfilled as you see the vision of His Kingdom-church.

King Jesus has big plans for His Kingdom. King Jesus called you by name to be part of His big plans. The most exciting time to be in His Kingdom-church is right now. Big things are about to happen, and those who are hungry and have faith will be the ones who will be a part of God's big plans to expand.

This is not the time to walk by sight and become fearful—because you will miss the miracles God has for you. To be part of God's big plans, you must think like God—*big*. Catch a big vision of yourself; be like Jesus. Catch a big vision of your church, the Kingdom-church. Catch the big vision of your ministry, not just church, but kingdom-realm ministry. When God's big vision captures your heart, then you will see God's big plans for you.

### The Fellowship of the King

In order for you to maximize your influence in your kingdom-realm, you must belong to the Fellowship of the King. This fellowship is two or more people bonded together with a common vision to become like King Jesus, invading, conquering, and plundering darkness. This vision is fulfilled as we relate together to achieve the common goal of making disciples by leading them into the Kingdom, so together you can become God-multipliers just like King Jesus. You have made disciples who are now following you, breaking through their barriers and maximizing their life for King Jesus.

You can begin a Fellowship of the King by giving *Maximize Your Influence* to others so they will catch the vision to become like Jesus—King Jesus—with you. Become the Fellowship of the King through bonding together by the vision of expanding the Kingdom of Heaven on the earth. Lead the fellowship to invade darkness, to achieve the goal to transform a victim of darkness in your kingdom-realm into a victor over darkness in the Fellowship of the Kingdom. This book will show you how to invade darkness before the return of King Jesus. Be with those who have a hunger and thirst that can be satisfied only by the invasion of the Spirit in their lives.

The other place to invade darkness: in church…

## A God-Multiplier in Church

When I entered the auditorium for first service, my eyes were drawn to a woman sitting alone with her head down. I sensed she was troubled, so I determined to talk with her when I was finished setting the Care Ministry in order. As I talked with a team leader, a lady named Dorothy approached me. Little did she know that she would bring the Kingdom of Heaven to earth; it was a natural moment transformed into a God-moment by availability.

Uncertainty was on her face as she smiled and related her story of how she arrived at this place at this time. "Some friends told me how much fun and how exciting the Care Ministry is, so I joined their team today." Then she told me why she was uncomfortable, "I haven't received any of the training they did. I don't know what to say, I don't know what to do, and I am scared!" But she was available.

Dorothy was a raw recruit for the Kingdom of Heaven. I smiled as Dorothy explained her trepidation. I smiled because she had broken through a stronghold (see 2 Cor. 10:4) that oppresses many mainte-nance-culture church members. The Bible says, "God has not given us a spirit of fear" (2 Tim. 1:7 NKJV), yet fear has invaded maintenance-culture churches to quench the ministry of the Spirit. Maintenance-culture members are afraid to talk to people, afraid of offending people, afraid to pray out loud, afraid of saying the wrong thing. Most use the word uncomfortable, but it is the spirit of fear. Satan has the people of God bound in fear so they cannot walk in the good works God has prepared for them. Fear has blinded their hearts so they do not recognize the God-moments in their lives.

Dorothy's availability demonstrated a spirit of faith instead of fear. Smiling, I said, "Dorothy, this ministry is simple. All you have to do is ask the three miracle-working questions: 'Hi, my name is Dorothy; what's your name? How long have you been coming here? Is there anything I can pray about with you?'"

Uncertainty changed to excitement when she heard how simple it was. She exclaimed, "I can do that!"

Then I directed her to where the Spirit of the Lord was waiting for her. I said, "Dorothy, there is a woman sitting alone, burdened down, why don't you go ask her the God-multiplying questions?"

As Dorothy walked toward the lady, she invaded the dominion of darkness oppressing her. Dorothy smiled at the lady, and said, "My name is Dorothy; what's your name?"

The lady responded, "My name is Claudia."

Then Dorothy asked, "How long have you been coming here?"

Claudia informed her, "Four weeks."

Sensing she was lonely, Dorothy asked, "Has anyone talked to you in those four weeks?"

Claudia responded by saying, "No one has."

Later, when I told this story to the staff, one defended the friendliness of the church by saying that he had talked with her. However, there is a difference between talking with someone and being available with the God-kind-of-heart. Claudia had been a miracle waiting to happen for four weeks, but no one made themselves available to love her and minister to her.

Dorothy invaded darkness and changed a natural moment into a God-moment when she asked, "Is there anything I can pray about with you?" Prayer is the invitation for the Spirit of God to invade. Dorothy wasn't with Claudia to be nice and friendly; she was with her to demonstrate God's love to lead her into God's Kingdom. Claudia began to weep because Dorothy's love conquered the lies of the enemy that told her that no one in church would authentically listen. Claudia told her through her tears, "My husband is institutionalized with drug dependence. He wants a divorce, and my son is in satan worship." First ministry Sunday, first person she ministered to, and Dorothy has a crisis on her hands!

This wounded soul sharing her need was God's moment for Dorothy. She conquered Claudia's fears with her faith, as she prayed for God to bring His Kingdom of peace into her troubled heart. Her prayer replaced the torment of fear upon Claudia's soul with an expectancy of God's salvation. This was her moment to be a miracle. Dorothy continued to demonstrate the love of God by staying with her and crying with her. Claudia sensed the compassion of the Father's heart. Dorothy opened her heart to Claudia, so Claudia could open her heart to King Jesus.

At the conclusion of the service Claudia indicated she wanted to receive the Lord, and Dorothy was with her. As they hugged and cried, Claudia told her, "I would have never responded this morning if you had not loved me before church." The love of God plundered the gates of hell that day, and Dorothy led a victim of darkness into the Kingdom of Heaven. Dorothy was a God-multiplier, just like Jesus. Claudia left church that day in the image of God, reflecting His love, forgiveness, and faith. He would invade her family with the dominion of God.

Dorothy invaded with the love of God. King Jesus interrupted the devil's plans for divorce, and He intruded into the dominion of darkness upon that family. Three months later Claudia's husband repented, entered into the Kingdom, and began to lead his family into the Kingdom of God. Three months later, her son did too. Dorothy became a God-multiplier. Three damaged souls were delivered out of darkness and received the rebirth from Heaven, and God expanded His heavenly Kingdom upon the earth.

This is the confession of faith we give to God-multipliers: "My availability gives God opportunity to be a miracle through me."

Dorothy maximized her influence when she:

— Made herself available to the Lord by faith.

— Made herself available to Claudia in love.

— Reflected the image of God to Claudia.

— Exerted Kingdom authority to interrupt the torment in Claudia's family.

— Expanded the Kingdom of Heaven into a family divided in darkness.

Dorothy became the "master" craftsman that day because she made a masterpiece by restoring God to the soul of Claudia. Each of us has unlimited influence in the Kingdom of God.

Often, I hear excuses come out of the mouths of good church members that are straight from the accuser: "You don't know the mess my life is in right now. God can't use me with this horrible mess. Someday I will serve the Lord, but right now I need Him to get me out of this mess."

The reason Dorothy wept with Claudia when she told her that her husband wanted a divorce is because she herself had received the Lord while going through the pain of betrayal and rejection of her messy divorce. Dorothy became the God-multiplier in Claudia's soul because her mess became a message of hope. Dorothy said, "Let me tell you how God healed my broken heart from my divorce."

*Your mess is your message and your test is your testimony!*

Dorothy maximized her influence because she did not allow the past to control her.

Dorothy maximized her influence by conquering her fears with faith.

Dorothy maximized her influence by plundering the kingdom of darkness of an entire family.

Dorothy maximized her life by increasing the capacity to receive from the Lord, for others' pain.

The adversary has been lying to you, disqualifying you from being a God-multiplier. Jesus the God-multiplier is in you! When you look at your life, you will disqualify yourself. When you look at your abilities, you will disqualify yourself. When you look at your past, you will disqualify yourself, but when you look at the Christ in you, the Anointed One in you, you will see the miracle is already there. You will see the God-multiplier.

There is a God-multiplier story in Luke 10:27-37, in the parable commonly referred to as "The Good Samaritan."

*And He* [King Jesus] *answering said, Thou shalt love the Lord thy God with all thy heart, and with all thy soul, and with all thy strength, and with all thy mind; and thy neighbour as thyself* (Luke 10:27).

*Neighbor* doesn't mean your next-door neighbor; it means the person who is "near" to you. Love the person near to you as you love yourself. The person near to you is the person you choose to have near to you. God-multipliers draw near, moved by compassion, to transform victims of darkness into victors over darkness. The God-multipliers see that their mission in life is to expand the Kingdom of Heaven on earth by destroying the works of the devil. The wounded man's life was transformed from a victim to victor because he received the love of the God-multiplier (the Samaritan who offered aide). The God-multiplier maximized his influence in this man's life because he made himself available to meet him at his point of need.

In this story we can see three spiritual conditions:

- A man journeyed away from the Lord to become a victim of darkness.

- Several men in the maintenance culture marginalized their influence.

- A man, a God-multiplier, maximized his influence.

The Samaritan became a God-multiplier on the earth because he was motivated by a God-kind-of-heart.

The God-kind-of-heart makes you a God-multiplier. "Blessed are the pure in heart, for they shall see God" (Matt. 5:8 NKJV).

- The God-multiplier saw the image of God, a masterpiece.

- The God-multiplier saw a God-moment to invade and plunder.

- The God-multiplier had an expectancy of the goodness of God and seized the opportunity to maximize his influence.

Why did Jesus choose a Samaritan to be the good guy? The Samaritans suffered in a culture that told them, "You are inferior." Their culture said, "You can't." Their culture told them to "Leave people alone, especially Jews; they don't like you. They think they are better than you. People don't want your love, care, and compassion. They don't want you invading their privacy. People want you to leave them alone."

Their culture said, "Be content that you are saved and going to Heaven. Don't believe you are a miracle. Don't believe you are on a journey where God gives you opportunities to be a miracle. Don't see God in this. These things happen. It is the natural course of life."

People get attacked on this road all the time. It happened just last week. The culture explains away the God-moments of life never to multiply God on the earth.

The Samaritan is the model of a God-multiplier who recognizes a divine moment, recognizing the need as an opportunity for God to do a miracle through him. The Samaritan earned the right to lead because he invested in the wounded man's life. He invested his time and invested his money. He made deposits of love to earn the right to lead to be a victor who rises above the limitations of culture, rises above the limitations of circumstances, rises above the rejection of those living marginalized lives. He rises above the setbacks and defeats of life by the power of a God-kind-of-heart to be a multiplier of God on the earth.

*And Jesus answering said, A certain man went down from Jerusalem to Jericho, and fell among thieves, which stripped him of his raiment, and wounded him, and departed, leaving him half dead* (Luke 10:30).

A certain man went down. This is a story not just about a natural event, but it also describes the spiritual path of a person who turns away from God. This man left Jerusalem, the city of God, and went down. He was not on the journey going higher to his destiny; he was going in the opposite direction—descending to Jericho. When you spiritually descend, your path inevitably will expose you to being robbed by evil forces of darkness (see John 10:10).

These spiritual thieves did not desire to kill him; they wanted him to live in torment. They wanted him to suffer the torment of knowing he missed it. They wanted to rob his self-confidence, rob his sense of value, rob him of his sense of righteousness. These demons wanted not only a wounded man, but a tormented soul.

A change point is when people encounter circumstances creating stress beyond their sense of control. He became a victim of darkness that brought him to a change point. He was in the valley of decision of whether he would respond to the Lord or, as a victim of darkness, succumb to the torment of his damaged soul and descend to a disabled life, never fulfilling his created purpose. This tormented soul was unable to hear the voice of God. His eyes were beaten shut, covered with doubt and unbelief, so they could not recognize the Spirit of God.

His damaged soul desperately needed a change-leader to lead him through this change point to his destiny.

*And by chance there came down a certain priest that way: and when he saw him, he passed by on the other side* (Luke 10:31).

"By chance" the priest "saw him," but he did not see God. He did not have the spiritual eyes to see the change-point opportunity to become the change-leader. He did not have eyes to see, nor did he have ears to hear. It was by chance, an inconvenient coincidence.

The priest was the most educated and trained individual to care for a wounded person, and the priest was in the most spiritually important position in the eyes of this man. If anyone could or would do what the Lord wanted him to do, it would be the priest. But the priest, despite his training and position, was not on the journey; he did not have eyes to see, nor ears to hear. He missed his God-moment to do what was important to God because he lacked compassion. So he sinned; he missed the path, missed the God-moment the Lord prepared for him to be a miracle.

*And likewise a Levite, when he was at the place, came and looked on him, and passed by on the other side* (Luke 10:32).

The Levite was the person who assisted the priest in the temple duties. In the church the Levite position would be the church council, elders, or board members. These are the people whom the church members look up to as very spiritual.

The board member came to the place of opportunity to be a miracle in someone's life, saw the need, knew the need, and passed by. He excused himself, "My life is just too busy to get involved with someone like that."

When you come to the place or moment of opportunity that the Lord gives you to be a miracle, and you pass it by on the other side, the Lord passes you by. You miss the Lord; and the more times you close your heart to compassion, the more you close the eyes of your heart to seeing the Lord.

*But a certain Samaritan, as he journeyed, came where he was: and when he saw him, he had compassion on him* (Luke 10:33).

The Samaritan came to the same "place" as the priest and Levite. The difference is that he had eyes to see; and what he saw was not a place to be avoided, but a God-moment! He was on that road not by chance, not by accident, but by appointment. He saw a person who should not to be ignored because of the inconvenience; instead he saw an opportunity to be available to God to invade with the love of God. He was to invade the moment with the compassion of God. He was there to interrupt the pain the evil one caused. He was to intrude to bring the Kingdom of Heaven to the wounded man.

The Samaritan had the same choice to make: to pass by on the other side or draw near. He had the same thoughts: "fiery darts" (Eph. 6:16) cast into his mind by the evil one, excuses to remain uninvolved, not to intrude in another person's affairs.

"After all, I'm just not that kind of person—that's just not me. I have never done anything like this before. Anyway, I don't have the time to get involved; I am so busy. I am busy with my family. I am busy at work. I am busy at church. I am busy, busy, busy." These are the thoughts of self-doubt that say that I can't really help someone.

The Samaritan's mind was probably filled with negative thoughts at the moment of choice: to risk being a miracle or remain in the security of mediocrity. However, he said no to his fears, no to unbelief, no to self-doubt, no to insecurity, no to the devil. And he said yes to God—yes to the God in him being a miracle through him, yes to the opportunity to change the eternal destiny of a wounded person, yes to the most fulfilling miracle of life—allowing love to draw near to another and become a God-multiplier.

When he recognized the moment, and he battled his own strongholds, and said yes to the Lord, at that moment, the Samaritan became a God-multiplier just like Jesus. He demonstrated love to the person in need. The God-multiplier made himself available because when he saw it, he recognized the moment, recognized the need, seized the opportunity to maximize his influence by bringing Kingdom of God to earth.

The Samaritan is an example of a God-multiplier on the journey because he was following the Lord to his destiny. His life was defined by how many God-moments he recognized. He was sensitive to the Spirit. When he saw the wounded man, he saw with the eyes of compassion and was motivated with the love of the Father.

*And went to him, and bound up his wounds, pouring in oil and wine, and set him on his own beast, and brought him to an inn, and took care of him* (Luke 10:34).

- The God-multiplier saw a victim beaten and left half-dead, but the eyes of faith saw a victor. He sowed his time and money, seeing the masterpiece in this damaged soul: This bloody half-dead victim of darkness will reflect the image of God, and he will exert dominion over the darkness that attempted to destroy him. He will fulfill the purpose for which he was created.

- The God-multiplier went to him because he was motivated by the compassion of the God-kind-of heart, not by convenience, nor by chance. Compassion moved him to draw near to be the neighbor of a victim. The Samaritan remembered when he was a victim of darkness, and he remembered the person who made himself available to be the change-leader in *his* life.

- The God-multiplier bound up his wounds. The wounds are places of separation—wounds upon the soul that separated this man from the vision and mission His Creator made for his life. The wounds were satan's attempt to damage and disable the victim's soul. The Samaritan maximized his love and compassion and brought back the hope of God's expected end. His faith for the victim to be a victor declared that God is the God of the second chance.

- The God-multiplier poured oil and wine upon his wounds. He anointed him with the Spirit to heal the broken heart, to set him free of his captivity, to proclaim the good news to the poor, and to proclaim the favorable year of the Lord (see Luke 4:18-19). And he poured the wine of joy upon his soul—the joy that comes from knowing that the God who created Heaven and earth knows you, loves you, and is healing your life. That joy came from the God-multiplier who invaded his life with the compassion of God.

- He set him on his beast. When he set him on his beast, the God-multiplier set him on *his journey*. This victim of darkness did not have the capacity to go on. If he was going to make it to the place of restoration of his soul, the God-multiplier had to take him there by carrying the victim out of darkness on his own journey to enable the wounded to get on his.

- Brought him on his journey. The word *brought* literally means to lead. It is the same word used to describe Jesus as the "finisher" of our faith—leader of our faith (see Heb. 12:2). Jesus is the chief and leader of our faith. The Samaritan led the wounded man back onto the journey of faith.

- To an inn. *Inn* comes from a word that means "a place of receiving all visitors or strangers." The inn is the Kingdom-church that receives strangers and visitors. In the Kingdom-church, strangers are received as important. Wounded victims are received seeing their creative potential.

- Why would Jesus, the chief change-leader, want us to take the wounded to the church? To be cared for by the church.

*And on the morrow when he departed, he took out two pence, and gave them to the host, and said unto him, Take care of him; and whatsoever thou spendest more, when I come again, I will repay thee* (Luke 10:35).

- "Take care of him": Jesus is bringing the wounded, disabled souls into our church because He sees the masterpiece within and commands us to take care of them.

- Investing in a victim with little sense of value, who does not feel as if they deserve the love, magnifies God's love above satan's wounds and is a deposit of love earning the right to become their change-leader.

- The Samaritan earned the right to influence the victim because he invested in him. He made himself available at the pain point to fill the wounds with the love and Spirit of God. He did not just impact the victim at the pain point, but continued the relationship when he returned.

- When the Samaritan returned he had earned the right to maximize his influence. Instead of a victim going in the wrong direction, he returned to find a disciple. He had earned the right to be the God-multiplier.

The Kingdom-church receives all the wounded, strangers, and visitors, because its mission is to expand the dominion of God over the victims within our kingdom-realm. It is the Kingdom-church mission for this half-dead victim to reflect the image of God. The Lord will increase the wounded being led to the Kingdom-church because He sees the manifestation of His love.

[Jesus asked:] *"Which now of these three, thinkest thou, was neighbour unto him that fell among the thieves?"* (Luke 10:36)

That is when he fulfilled the second commandment.

*And he said, He that showed mercy on him. Then said Jesus unto him, Go, and do thou likewise* (Luke 10:37).

The word Jesus used for "go" means to pursue the journey, or lead the journey; lead one to pursue the journey. There are those who go through life but never pursue the journey, and never lead anyone else on the journey. The change-leader hears the Lord Jesus command him to "go on your journey" and discover the divine appointment.

Jesus employed the same word "go and do likewise" here as He did in Matthew 28:19, when He issued a parallel command: "Go...and make disciples." Here it tells us how to go and make disciples. He said, "Go make a disciple by earning the right to be a change-leader, so you can lead them to pursue the journey with you."

When you believe you have a destination, when you believe all men have a destination, when you believe the enemy battles you to stop you from reaching the destination for which you were born, then you will become a God-multiplier.

On the journey you have eyes to see. On the journey you have ears to hear. When you are not on the journey accidents happen, and life is by chance. The journey is defined by the God-moments, and the Lord leads you to those people He wants you to impact.

We must earn the right to influence people to follow us. Influencing people is the key to leadership. Earning the right is the key to ministry. You earn the right to influence people so you can lead them.

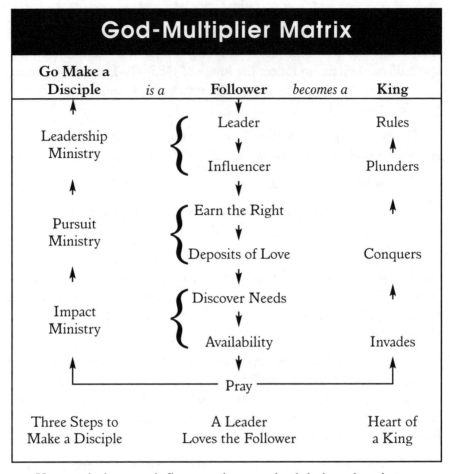

| Go Make a Disciple | *is a* | Follower | *becomes a* | King |
|---|---|---|---|---|
| Leadership Ministry | { | Leader ↓ Influencer | | Rules ↑ Plunders |
| Pursuit Ministry | { | Earn the Right ↓ Deposits of Love | | ↑ Conquers |
| Impact Ministry | { | Discover Needs ↓ Availability | | ↑ Invades |
| | | Pray | | |
| Three Steps to Make a Disciple | | A Leader Loves the Follower | | Heart of a King |

You maximize your influence when you lead darkened souls to magnify God on this earth by reflecting His image and exerting His authority. This matrix has three movements:

We begin with what Jesus commanded us to make: a disciple.

The center row begins with follower because a disciple is a follower.

Now we will work down the row. We begin at the top because we begin with the end in mind.

A disciple is a: Follower.

To be a follower, you need a: Leader.

*How do you become a leader in someone's heart?*

You become a person of: Influence.

To be a person of influence: Earn the Right.

You earn the right to influence when you make: Deposits of Love.

You make deposits of love by: Being Available.

You become available to God in: Prayer.

Being a leader in someone's life begins simply by "drawing near." Being available to make deposits of love earns you the right to influence them to follow you.

Moving up the right side of the matrix: Invading darkness to plunder.

Invade darkness: availability to recognize God-moments to seize the moment.

Conquer darkness: discover the need and meet victims at their point of need.

Plunder: earn the right to lead them into the Kingdom.

Rule: lead the new disciple to invade their kingdom-realm.

# 10

# MAXIMIZE YOUR INFLUENCE: MAKE A DISCIPLE

Why make a disciple? King Jesus declared the mission for those who desire to maximize their influence on this earth: "Go therefore and make disciples" (Matt. 28:19 NKJV). The vision of those following Jesus is to go on their breakthrough journey of life and make followers. Compel others to follow you to their breakthrough journey. Making disciples is being like King Jesus, the God-multiplier.

With 95 percent of all Christians barren, the devil has stolen Christians' capacity to maximize their influence. Controlled by fear and distracted by the cares of life, disciples of King Jesus must break through satanic barriers to maximize their influence and transform the life of those oppressed in darkness. Followers of King Jesus are afraid to follow Him outside the church building to minister to those in darkness, so why don't we start the breakthrough journey in the building by ministering to those coming to church oppressed by darkness: the visitors. The easiest place to stretch outside of our comfort zone is in church. The easiest place to mentor and model the ministry is in church, and the easiest place to pray for those wounded by darkness is in church. Let's begin attacking darkness when it walks in the church door.

The visitors who attend your church are the first opportunity for you to be a God-multiplier. Here is an illustration:

Julie, trained in the Care Ministry to recognize God-moments by the seven stop signs of hurting people, was greeting people in the foyer. Lisa, a visitor, walked in, so Julie approached her and began to talk with her. Julie had ears to hear the pain in the other woman's voice, so she asked, "Why are you here today?" Lisa responded, "I am looking for a church home." Julie persisted, sensing Lisa was hurting, "I mean, why are you here?" Lisa began to cry when she explained by saying, "I lost my job." When Julie heard the motivating need, the pain point, she was able to meet Lisa's need by praying with her, loving her, and sitting with her during church. When they told me their story a couple of months later, they were best friends, and Lisa was multiplying God on a Care Team because her heart-felt needs were met by the Care Ministry.

Some may object to Julie's invasion of Lisa's anonymity. Others may say, "I would be offended if someone approached me that way." Here is why it did not offend Lisa. First, she had a need. Julie was sensitive to Lisa, not just to protect her, but to love her. She recognized the need; she had eyes to see and ears to hear. I know this may be a novel idea, but Julie was actually led by the Spirit to meet Lisa at her pain point—in church! Because Julie recognized the God-moment, the Spirit elevated the ministry beyond the natural ability of Julie.

Julie was intrusive—intruding, praying against, the devil's plans of poverty for Lisa. Yes, Julie was invasive—invading the devil's oppression of fear and worry. Yes, Julie was interruptive—she interrupted the devil depression and replaced it with faith and hope imparted to Lisa through Julie's prayer.

Why? The Lord led Lisa to church that Sunday because He wanted to invade her life with His compassion to meet her at her point of need. He wanted to interrupt her discouragement with His hope. He wanted to intrude upon her fears with His faith. He wanted to destroy the works of the devil. That is why He led Lisa to church that day. It was a God-moment, not with Julie, but for Lisa to meet God.

How did Lisa receive her God-moment in church? God draws people to Himself. Lisa drove by the church, and the Spirit of God said to her, "Go to church and you will meet Me in My house." She drove by again, and again the Spirit spoke to her, "Come to My house and you will meet Me in My house." Weeks went by and, finally, Lisa walked into church. She went there to meet God. Why would she expect to meet God at His house? She had an appointment to meet God.

Julie's availability to be led by the Spirit stretched her comfort zone to reach out to a stranger. When Julie made herself available to Lisa to listen with compassion, Lisa received her God-moment when the Kingdom of Heaven invaded her life. At that moment God overruled the kingdom of darkness, and the evil forces tormenting Lisa were defeated. At that moment Lisa joined the journey to her destination.

Churches bound in the maintenance culture will never have the capacity for their visitors to experience their God-moments. Maintenance-culture churches don't even know God has moments in their church. People like Lisa will never find God's compassion in the maintenance culture because the maintenance-church members do not have the eyes of faith to recognize those the Lord leads to their church. They think visitors are there by chance. They do not believe the Lord will lead damaged and disabled victims of darkness to meet Him in His house, to free them from the oppression of the devil.

There is a battle for Lisa's soul. The enemy hates when victims of darkness attend church because that is where the Kingdom of God is to be manifested and they should be delivered out of his oppressive control. So what the devil has done is deceive the church into thinking that they offend people when looking for divine appointments, when they are as sensitive to the Spirit as they are to people. When you *believe* that people who attend oppressed should be set free, when you believe people come to church discouraged and leave with hope, then people come to church sick and leave whole. The church is the place where the work of the enemy is destroyed. The church is where the Kingdom of Heaven is to be manifested on the earth. If anyone is to see the Kingdom of Heaven, go be with people who name the name above every other name—the name of Jesus.

Visitors do not need anonymity. They need authenticity. They desperately need an authentic God who demonstrates His compassion for them. They need a God who cares about them and will let them know His love. Visitors need authentic followers of King Jesus to be as sensitive to the Spirit of God as they are to them. Visitors do not need to have Christian "Levites" passing by on the other side. They don't need pastors viewing visitors as chance attenders. Visitors need God. They need a disciple of Jesus who will be moved by compassion, become available to the Spirit of God and to the wounded, to earn the right to influence them by the love and Spirit of God.

How was Lisa transformed from a wounded person to one who has joined the journey? How did she encounter the Lord in church through Julie? There is an intentional ministry empowering Christians to become God-multipliers, destroying the works of the devil, by making themselves available to be sensitive to both people and God. That ministry is described in my first book: *You Are a Miracle—Waiting to Happen.* Since 1987 we have seen the Spirit of God keep His divine appointments through ordinary Christians who chose to be like Jesus—leading them on the journey.

Visitors are not visitors—visitors are miracles disguised as needs.

Why would anyone waste a perfectly good Sunday morning to sleep in, and instead get up early and spend three hours of their greatest asset—time—to attend your church? Why would someone risk going to a strange church with strange worship and strange people? Because they have a need!

The church in the maintenance culture will transform lives of hurting visitors only by accident not by intentionality. Hurting people, like Lisa, will never find God's compassion in the maintenance-culture church that does not believe the Lord will lead people to His church to discover His love and the freedom from the oppression of the devil.

## Transforming Visitors to First-Time Attenders (FTA)

The first step to transforming victims of darkness into disciples of King Jesus is to transform them from a visitor into an FTA (a First-Time Attender). They will never become a miracle in the house of God as a visitor. If a victim of darkness walks into your church as a visitor, a stranger, and walk out as a visitor, they will never become a disciple of King Jesus.

A *visitor* is a number, just a warm body on campus. The Care Ministry has a goal to transform visitors or guests into First-Time Attenders:

1. Someone you can identify on the church campus.

2. Someone you can make a relational connection with.

3. Someone for whom you can discover a motivating need.

4. Someone with whom you can earn the right to continue the relationship.

A visitor, or FTA, is a victim of darkness, even the Christians who are looking for a "church home." They are victims first because they are deceived in thinking they only need a church home. Getting a church home will be a counterfeit experience for them to experience the breakthrough journey the Lord has for them. Church homes are what church members have in the maintenance culture. The church home is the deception of the maintenance culture. Instead, they need a relationship with a disciple of King Jesus who will lead them to become victors in the Kingdom of Heaven.

FTAs are victims of the darkness in this world because they have no spiritual covering. If church members have left their church either because they didn't like the new carpet, or the air conditioning was set too cold, they are spiritually uncovered. If they have moved and are looking for a new church home, they are spiritually uncovered and open to distraction into the things of this world. Their spiritual discipline weakens, their prayers weaken, and they lose spiritual dynamic. They do not have the covering and reward of a man of God, the person who stands in the office of pastor.

They are a victim because they have needs that can be met in the Kingdom, the rule of God coming into their lives. They do not need a church home; they need King Jesus to invade their darkness with His authority and anointing to destroy the works of the devil.

## DO YOUR VISITORS EXPERIENCE THE AMERICAN OR BIBLICAL MINISTRY PARADIGM?

Culture is the spirit or attitude of your church members that victims of darkness intuit when they walk into your building. They can feel the spirit of your church. Is it a church that desires to meet strangers at their point of need, or is it a church that is self-focused?

The maintenance culture is one of the first dynamics that victims of darkness perceive from your church members. When your church members attend church to maintain their church programs and church relationships, while ignoring victims of darkness as unimportant or insignificant, visitors may not be able to verbalize what they feel, but they have encountered the maintenance culture. They feel unimportant and unwanted, and will probably never return.

When the pastor views the FTAs as unimportant and does not invest in his future church every Sunday, the victims are impacted by the maintenance culture. If the attitude toward the FTAs who take the time and effort to attend your church is that they are unimportant, how much more insignificant are the victims of darkness to your church members?

The behavior of the church members in the maintenance culture is that they invest their time and money to maintain their church member life and their church. Maintenance culture is the attitude motivating church members to be satisfied in maintaining what they have. They have no compassion nor time for the victims of darkness whom the Holy Spirit leads to them so that they can meet the victim at their point of need and lead them on the breakthrough journey. Church members are not on the journey, so they have no interest in the wounded on the side of the road.

The American paradigm says FTAs want their space.

The biblical paradigm says victims of darkness have needs that motivate them to look for God and make them hungry for the Spirit.

The American paradigm says people want anonymity.

The biblical paradigm says the wounded FTA wants authenticity.

The American paradigm says it takes time for people to become receptive to the gospel of the Kingdom.

The biblical paradigm says it takes a God-moment.

The American paradigm says Christians are ineffective in ministry.

The biblical paradigm says to love your neighbor—every believer is a leader.

The American paradigm says people don't want to have relationships.

The biblical paradigm says everyone needs the love of God.

## A SPECIFIC MINISTRY TO VISITORS

Why does the church need a specific ministry to visitors?

Often people are led by the Spirit to attend church "oppressed by the devil" with needs they cannot meet. Therefore, they attend church during a change point in their life looking for God to meet their need.

The church is the entrance to the Kingdom of Heaven on the earth. When people attend church with discouragement, they should leave with hope. They attend church oppressed by the devil; they leave knowing the freedom in Christ Jesus. When victims of darkness walk into the church, they walk into a different atmosphere. They have left the darkness of the world and have entered into the dynamic of Heaven. They have entered into a place where the love of God is manifested through those who are disciples of King Jesus. They enter into the peace found only in the Kingdom of God. They enter into the place where praise brings joy. It is different because the church brings the government of God to earth.

When hurting, oppressed people attend church but do not meet God—do not have a God-moment with His love and Spirit meeting them at their point of need—when victims do not discover the compassion of the Father's heart in the heart of a disciple of the King to lead them on their journey out of darkness into the Kingdom, then the enemy comes to them to deceive them, not about their relationship with the church, but about God. He tells them God does not care about them. They are not important to God. God cannot help them. They leave church with an opinion about themselves: I am not good enough for God. God does not love me, and God will not help me.

When they leave church with that impression of God and of themselves, the enemy kidnaps them from church. They quit looking for God to help them. They quit being open to God during their change point, and they are deceived by the kingdom of darkness for their help. When someone approaches them about church, they respond, "I tried God; I went to church."

Something is wrong when hurting oppressed people attend a church with the name of Jesus on it, and they do not find the love of God. They do not find the Spirit of God. They do not find hope. Instead they find people who ignore them, and they come to the conclusion: God is not in this place.

The enemy wants to kidnap them from the Kingdom of God. He does not want them to meet God in church, he does not want them to experience the love of God, and he does not want them to experience the ministry of the Spirit. He wants them to experience a natural church that has no more answers than any other institution he controls.

- The church must have a ministry specifically designed to meet the needs of the wounded victims of the darkness in this world who attend church as "visitors," "guests," or whatever name we use. What we call them does not matter, but how we meet them at their point of need does.

- The church is the change agent on the earth. We exist to make disciples for Jesus. When strangers attend our church, our goal is not for them to have a church home, but to become disciples, followers on the journey with us. Our goal must be a disciple of Jesus Christ.

- A disciple of Jesus Christ does not join a church; he/she has relationships in the church in order to make disciples. It takes a disciple to make a disciple. It takes someone on the journey to lead others on the journey. That is why it is significant to determine what a disciple is, so we can begin making disciples.

The flash point for the clash of the kingdoms is in the church when oppressed people walk in, disconnected, disjointed. The church is where the conflict occurs for the souls of men. When FTAs attend church, the battle has begun. They have entered into the place where the Kingdom of Heaven dwells upon the earth. They are looking for a different kingdom. They are looking for God to invade their life. The church is where the clash of the kingdoms is to occur—where people are delivered out of the kingdom of darkness into the Kingdom of Heaven. It is not a place to get people to have a church home.

## THE IMPACT MINISTRY

The Impact Ministry meets the needs of victims of darkness by the Spirit and love of God. It is the first step to make a disciple because you must "earn the right" to lead someone into the Kingdom. Demonstrating the compassion of the King by being aware of and sensitive to the Spirit and to their needs meets them at their pain point and impacts their heart.

The Impact Ministry begins with the heart filled with the faith to be available to God to be a miracle in their life. It is the faith to believe this natural moment of time enters into the transcendency of eternity because my availability will be a God-moment for the Kingdom of Heaven to invade someone else's need through me. This victim of darkness will never be the same after having their encounter with the King and His Kingdom through me. I am invading whatever darkness satan has placed in their lives with the love and power of God to free them from that oppression.

The reason church members are unavailable is because they are in unbelief. The Impact Ministry is the first step to earn the right to lead them on the journey to their destination.

## CHURCH IMPACT MINISTRY DEFINED

The church application of the Impact Ministry is that the ministry must meet the unique needs of the visitors. Many church members' attitudes are, "We meet the needs of the visitors by meeting the needs of members." But by only meeting the needs of your members you will miss God's opportunity to minister to your future church. Unique needs present unique opportunities and require intentional ministry.

*And when Jesus came to the place, He looked up, and saw him, and said unto him, Zacchaeus, make haste, and come down; for to day I must abide at thy house* (Luke 19:5).

Zacchaeus heard about King Jesus, and wanted to see Him, but he could not because people were between him and Jesus. How many times are the same people who should be available to the Lord to bring others to Him are the ones who are interfering with wounded people finding Him?

Because he could not get to King Jesus, Zacchaeus climbed up a sycamore tree, waiting to see Him. When Jesus passed by that place, He looked up. (It is an unnatural physical movement to look up, but Jesus was sensitive to the Spirit to look for a God-moment.)

When He saw him, He declared to this man hiding in the tree, "Zacchaeus, I must be with you today." That is what Jesus is saying through you to the wounded in your life: "I must be with you today."

Why do you have such a focus on the FTA? Because the FTA are wounded, looking for Jesus, so they climb into the tree of your church to see if King Jesus would pass by their life—to see if He would care, to see if Jesus would notice them in your church. They feel small and feel insignificant. They don't know why you even want to talk to them. They just want to see Jesus pass by. The wounded ignored by church members are the very people that Jesus stops, looks upon, and says, "I must be with you today."

Why do we focus on the FTA? Because God leads them to church to experience His Kingdom in your church. They are there to be impacted by the Spirit. When Jesus passes them by He will look at them through you, and He will say, "I must be with you today." It will take a while before you have that sense of a God-moment occurring. At the beginning you will see it after it happens, but eventually, you will hear the Spirit say, "I must be with them today."

You may be saying: *Why don't you give people the space to gradually process from liking the church to attending church to serving in the church? Don't you know people need their space?* The problem with the present system is that it does not make disciples of Jesus Christ. We stop looking for God-moments. We stop being sensitive to the wounded the Lord brings to our church. We stop looking up to see the insignificant. We become insensitive to the Spirit, insensitive to hurting people, and miss hearing Jesus say to us, "I must be with you today."

Will we alienate people because we are so intrusive? Love is not intrusive. Disciples of King Jesus can be taught the skills of love to invite victims of darkness to be open with their needs and, more importantly, open to God's invading their needs with His power and love. The Holy Spirit is gentle. The fruit of the Spirit is gentleness. We do not force people to become our friends; we do not force people to pray. Love invites people to share their needs with us, so the Spirit of God can meet them at their point of need.

Let's say that one Sunday a visitor attends the church and a God-multiplier approaches them to minister to them, but just the question offends, and they turn around and walk right out of church. Let's say they are really angry, and they call the pastor on Monday to complain that someone wanted to pray with them in church:

"Pastor Smith, I want you to know I attended your church yesterday, and I was offended because someone in your church wanted to pray with me."

Pastor Smith says, "Sir, I deeply regret that we did anything that would offend anyone at our church. I do have a solution for you. I will give you the names and telephone numbers of ten churches that will not pray for you when you attend their church."

The spirit of fear has been breeding mistrust into the minds and hearts of people for decades. In the 1980s many televangelists fell, and the message was, "You can't trust preachers; all they want is your money." Then in the 1990s the many lies of politicians were exposed, and the message again was, "You can't trust politicians." Then in 2000, corporate executives were exposed as greedy men, and again the message is, "You cannot trust executives."

So when people attend your church, they have a question floating in the back of their mind, "Can I trust these people? Do they just want to use me and not care about me?" The first obstacle we must overcome is the obstacle of fear and mistrust.

The other question they have is, "Do I like this church?" One of the most significant factors to whether they like the church or not is how people in the church relate to them—as much as the public presentation. People want to be with people who love, accept, and appreciate them. That is why pre-service and post-service have as much impact as the service itself.

You only have one chance to make a first impression. That is why the church must have a ministry dedicated to the FTA, so they will discover that the love of God and the Spirit of God abides in this house.

What about the people who are not wanting to pray with someone and are not wanting to begin a relationship? What about people who just want to attend church and want to hide because of past hurts? While I have compassion upon their pain, hiding in church, disconnected from the Body, is the slowest way to heal. Healing occurs as you walk in the light.

We are not serving people by allowing their fears to control them. What is the solution to distrustful people who think, "I must be careful not to let this church use me"? What is the solution to fearful people who think, "I must not let this church hurt me"? For their sake we cannot leave them alone. We cannot allow their fears to control our behavior. Whenever fear controls, it is destructive. So what is our proactive response?

"Love casts out fear." Victims of darkness do not attend church looking for anonymity; they are looking for authenticity. They are desperately looking for an authentic disciple of King Jesus to demonstrate the love in the Kingdom and the power of the Kingdom. They are looking for someone to accept them, discover their value and appreciate them, want to be with them, and invite them to belong. That is true with all of us.

What does it mean to be authentic?

First, it is making a decision that this stranger, this victim of darkness is the most important person to me in the whole world. It is being totally there with them. It is making them feel important because of the attention I give. It is communicating by focusing my spirit, soul, and body to say, "I am here for you." My spirit is activated by faith to hear what the Spirit would say to me. My soul is activated by compassion to care for them, and my body is totally there with them through body language. These are skills of love that invite them to encounter God. Being authentic is sharing their pain with them; it is inviting them to feel accepted by sharing a similar experience.

## EXCUSES FOR DISENGAGEMENT

*The fear of offense.* Often people ask, "What if I offend them by something that I do or say?" My response is that the church has been offensive by not doing anything and not saying anything. The real offense is to the Spirit of God because we do not follow the biblical rules of engagement.

*"I do not know how to be led by the Spirit. I do not know how to communicate love effectively."* The only thing you can do if that is you is *grow!* Invest in your relationship with God so you can impact people.

*"That's just not me."* If you think you just don't have the personality to impact someone's eternal destiny, then all I have to say to you is *change!* Don't allow your past experiences dictate to you what your future and destiny will be. Practice the skills of love. Practice the skills of the Spirit. Invest in yourself. Focus on this area of your life so you can become an effective God-multiplier. At the end of your life when you are entering into eternity, the only thing that will matter is *did you multiply God on the earth?*

Personal attention cannot drive people away. The people who complain about getting too much attention are the people who have decided this is not the church for them. So any giving to them will be over the top. They don't want anything from you, so therefore, leave them alone. The people who like the church welcome the attention. The people who are in the middle will appreciate the attention and care, and it may draw them back to a church where the public presentation may not be what they were looking for.

If I do not want to belong, then I won't. If I did not like my experience, and I have decided I am going somewhere else, then any attention I receive from the church is too much. What is over the top? How much attention is too much? How much ministry is too much? How much demonstration of love and acceptance is too much?

It all depends upon the God-multiplier's heart and attitude. If the attitude is, "We must make you a member of the church," or if the attitude is one of using people, then that attitude will be communicated through the actions and tone of voice, and even the words we use will be motivated by the attitude that "We want you to belong to our church."

---

The most important response to providing too much of a good thing is our attitude. If I authentically care about them, and my attitude is not to make them part of my church but to authentically desire God to invade their pain point, then that heart attitude will be sensed by the wounded soul and they will receive from me. If I have loved someone, cared for them and their oppression, then I have earned the right to take another step to make them a disciple.

If I have done that with gentleness, love, and kindness, then searching hearts will be opened. Fearful hearts will be opened. Hurting hearts will be opened. The real question is, how many lives have we impacted today? How many hearts were opened by the love of God today? How many lives were changed today? Our mission is to make disciples, not make members. The most important aspect of ministry is authenticity. Being honest, open, and transparent with those damaged souls will invite them to trust us. The extent to which we open our heart is the same extent they will open theirs.

## How Can We Complete This Mission?

The question isn't how many visitors attended this morning, nor is it whether or not they enjoyed the service, because disciples will never be made by worship service enjoyment. The question is how many victims began the breakthrough journey today to become victors by our love and ministry bonding them to the God-multiplier? How open is their heart and mind to following us out of the darkness into the Kingdom of God? The goal we must have for each FTA is to transform FTAs into disciples of King Jesus, victors who are followers of Him in the journey.

The first question is: How did Care Members fulfill their mission of becoming an influencer today? How many practiced the skills of love and the Spirit today? How many loved victims of darkness to earn the right to pray for them?

The question should be about my behavior and my heart. How many wounded was I able to authentically care for today? How many FTAs did I impact today? Have I earned the right to take the next step with them?

Our ministry Sunday mission is to begin the relationship, to discover needs, to demonstrate compassion, to pray with them, to have them know the presence of God. The important question is: Have they begun the journey with us? It is not: Were we a friendly church? It is not: Did they get so many touches? It is not: Did they have a good first impression? Asking those questions will miss the real objective of invading darkness with the Kingdom of Heaven. Have we influenced them enough to take the next step on their breakthrough journey?

## RECOGNIZE WHO THE HURTING PEOPLE ARE IN THE MEETING

If we are going to impact visitors, we must know where they are located in the meeting. If we do not know who the victims of darkness are, nor do we know where they are seated, then we cannot take the first step in making them feel important to us, and making them feel like they matter to us. So identifying the visitors is the first step in making them FTAs.

## DISCOVER AND MEET NEEDS

The power of the enemy's oppression is in the darkness of the silent soul. The power begins to be broken when it is brought to the light. Darkness become light when brought to the light. The healing process begins when the hurting person shares their burden with a disciple of King Jesus who authentically love them and believe with them for God's Kingdom to come and God's will to be done for them.

That is the power of love. Love invites FTAs to give their burden to the Lord in a very real way when they share it with a God-multiplier. The burden is lifted off (see Isa. 10:27), and the oppression is freed when a God-multiplier prays Heaven to earth.

## ONCE YOU HAVE EARNED THE RIGHT, PURSUE THE RELATIONSHIP TO JOIN THE JOURNEY

The first step you take with a victim of darkness is to be authentic with them so they will share with you their motivating need—the need that motivated them to church. That God-moment, when they tell of how darkness has oppressed them, is their heart opening to their break-through journey when you know your mission—is to multiply God by making a disciple. The mission of church members is to be nice, the mission of God multipliers is to make a disciple—someone following you on the breakthrough journey to their destination.

The purpose of beginning the relationship is actually the entry point to join the breakthrough journey. The journey is never traveled alone. Often people attempt to follow King Jesus on their own, and it ends in defeat, or is at best a very halting, slow, delayed process to their destination, and they never become the complete vision the Lord has for them.

The purpose of the encounter with the love and Spirit of God in church is to lead the hurting person to the path of the journey. That journey begins by a choice to become a disciple—a follower of King Jesus.

The vision is to make victims into disciples following God-multipliers into the Kingdom of God on their own breakthrough journey. Pre-service and post-service personal ministry to the FTA has as a great an impact on victims joining the journey as the public ministry of preaching and worship. If the objective is for "guests" of the Sunday morning service to have a wonderful "church experience" and to return next week, and the only objective of the church is for "guests" to attend meetings and the size of attendance is the ultimate goal, then the church does not need relationships. If the goal is to make disciples of King Jesus on the journey to our destination together, then relationships of love are the genesis of our Kingdom experience.

The key to success is to find a need and fill it. Find a hurt and heal it—that is what love does. Love meets needs. Love heals hurts.

The enemy has oppressed this world with poverty, sickness, and brokenness. There are needs all around us because darkness is all around us.

## IMPACT MINISTRY PRINCIPLES

Visitors attend church with one question: Is this the church that will meet my needs? They are oppressed in this dark world, and they do not have the answers to their needs.

The Spirit's mission is to draw oppressed victims out of the kingdom of darkness. The church is the entrance to experience the government of God on the earth, and the Spirit leads people to the Church so they will be delivered out of darkness.

Some important considerations are:

- The enemy hates the Church and will sabotage its mission of deliverance.

- The battle for souls of men must be engaged the first Sunday victims attend.

- The enemy wants to kidnap them out of the Kingdom back into darkness.

- The maintenance-culture church is ineffective because it does see the need, nor the battle, and is therefore prepared only for defeat every Sunday.

- *Visitors make up their minds in the first 11 minutes if they are coming back or not.*

## HOW THE MAINTENANCE CULTURE FAILS THE MISSION

My family was kidnapped by evil forces because of the ill-prepared and ill-equipped maintenance culture church. As I traveled in ministry, my wife was searching for a church home. We had three teenagers at the time and we had some big needs. I traveled, so I needed spiritual covering. My kids were teenagers, so they needed relationships during this time. And my wife was needing a champion in the journey. We were a miracle disguised as a need.

She was invited to a church by the Christian school administrator where she was office secretary. She attended three weeks and told me she thought this might be our church home. I looked on my calendar for an open weekend and determined to go as a family on that Sunday to place membership.

Cheryl had heard that they offered a class for teenagers during the second service, so we decided to attend that service to get our kids in that class. We knew teenagers would not want to attend a church if they felt alone and unaccepted.

When we arrived at the church we knew there was a class, but we did not know where, so I was going to get directions to the class. The only problem was that there was no one to ask at the door, so we walked down a long hallway and encountered a lady in the hall who was taking names for the nursery. I walked up to her and asked her, "Where is the class for the teenagers?"

She looked up at me, shrugged her shoulders, and responded, "I don't know, but I think it's down that way." That did not help because that was the only direction the hallway went. So I said, "Thank you." And we continued down this hallway, lost.

Then we came to a group of people talking to themselves and ignoring us. The more they ignored us, the more I felt they did not care about us. They did not care about my family. They did not care about our needs. I came to that conclusion because if they would have cared, they would have demonstrated it. They demonstrated that they were interested in their friends and their lives, but not about me and my family. The more they ignored us, the more I wondered if we wanted this to be our church, and the more I questioned if I really wanted to place church membership with them.

We finally arrived at the class for teenagers. You know how teenagers love to go to new situations? My kids did not want to go into that class full of strangers. So they turned their back to the door. I said to them, "This is your class; it is time for you to go on in." My son, who is as big as I am, said, "Dad, we don't want to go to this class." And my two daughters were standing behind him and said, "That's right, Dad, we don't want to go." I realized I had a mutiny on my hands.

I responded by giving them information they already had, "We came to this service for you to attend this class, so go to class." That did not motivate them. My son said, "Dad, we don't want to go." I said, "You are going"; he said, "No." I said, "Yes"; he said, "No"...

During this intelligent conversation, teenagers would walk by my kids ignoring them as they entered into the classroom. If anyone would have stopped and said, "Why don't you come on in?", everything would have been fine, but the entire morning no one helped, no one cared.

Finally, I had to pull rank on my kids, "Get into the class." They joyfully went into the class. By now I am disappointed. My family needed the church to help us, and we were finding no help. My family needed the church to care about us, and it did not. My family needed a church to love us, and it would not.

As my wife and I entered the sanctuary, we continued to be ignored, and we continued to feel unimportant. After a song, they invited people to greet the person next to you. One person greeted us; he had been there for six months and he didn't know anyone either. Right then I said, "I'm not coming back. I don't care if Jesus shows up, I am not coming back." Two things did not happen that Sunday. First, Jesus did not show up. Second, I don't remember what the preacher preached about, and it did not matter, because the decision was already made.

I needed a church to care about my teenagers to motivate them to be a part. My wife and I needed a sense that someone cared about us and our family. It was a disappointing experience of the maintenance culture. We attended this church to place membership, but they didn't want us, they didn't care about us, and we were unimportant to them.

We wanted to be tithing, serving, and involved members of the church, but in this the Scripture saying is true, "Having eyes they do not see, and having ears they do not hear." This church missed the God-moment for my family that Sunday because they did not see. When we left the church, the enemy was waiting for my family, telling my teenage children they did not need church to have a relationship with God, telling me that churches do not know how to relate to para-church organizations and that churches would not be concerned about me or my family. How many families have left your church only to be kidnapped by evil forces of darkness because of a church's failure to demonstrate the love and power of the Kingdom of God with the question, "Who needs to be a part of something as unloving as the church?"

The anointing upon the pastor can be wasted if the anointing is not upon the members to be God-multipliers. Negative experiences prior to the worship service close the hearts of the FTA to the public presentation.

How many churches do not have God-multipliers empowered with ministry skills, and do not have their church equipped with the ministry models to meet the needs of the victims who attend their church? They miss the opportunity to expand the Kingdom of God, and they miss the moment to change the destiny of the hurting people. Once again, the enemy kidnaps them out of the Kingdom of Heaven, and they never know the love of God. They never know God's vision and mission for their life.

11

# CHANGE YOUR CULTURE

The greatest need in the church is for church members to be motivated beyond maintenance of their lives. Most pastors are unable to motivate their members because of familiarity and they are embedded in the maintenance culture. It does not require 100 percent involvement to change the culture, which is good news since a church can't get 100 percent involvement in a free Sunday dinner.

Changing from maintenance culture to Kingdom-culture requires a critical mass of only 20 percent of your congregation. For this 20 percent to be the critical mass to move the church to a higher level, they must be motivated by a common vision, mission, and values to achieve the same goals. They will unite together in prayer for the common battle; they will model the new behavior of the Kingdom-culture, then the church will change.

Why does it require 20 percent of your congregation to effectively make disciples from FTAs? It takes a class to make a church member, but it takes a disciple to make a disciple. Relationships of love are the only way anyone becomes part of the Body of Christ. Attending meetings does not make you part of the Body. Building a relationship that earns the right to influence another person to the level of them wanting to become part of the Body requires four to six weeks.

# THREE PRE-SERVICE FTA DEPOSITS OF LOVE

## 1. Make the FTA Important

The objective of our ministry to the FTA is to open their heart so they may receive all of the Kingdom of Heaven in your church. When people attend your church, they are there in hope—hoping to find God for their life. If they did not have a need, they would not waste the time attending your church. They are looking for some sign that this is the place the Lord is directing them to attend.

The easiest step for Christians to invade darkness with the Kingdom of Heaven on the earth is to care about the victims who walk onto our church campus. If Christians do not overcome their fears and do not have the confidence to talk to the people who attend their church, how will they ever have the confidence to talk to someone outside of the church building?

The first step the FTA takes into your church you want to Wow them. As one mother of a Care Ministry member told me, "Every time I go to my daughter's church I feel like royalty." That is exactly what you want every FTA to feel like—Wow, I am important—because everyone wants to be with the people you feel important to. Love will draw people back to your church when your public presentation is less than or different from what they want.

## 2. Make Friends With the FTA

The second way to demonstrate the love of God is to become their friend. The best friend you will ever have is the person the Lord touches through you. The best friend you will ever have is the one you lead them out of the barrenness of their need into the abundance of the Kingdom of Heaven.

That goal is for every FTA to have one new friend the first Sunday they attend. You want them leaving your church feeling like they are important to someone, feel like someone cares about them, has heard them, accepts them, likes them, and will continue to pray for them. You want them leaving having a reason to return—the motivation to return is the love of God.

### 3. Meet the Needs of the FTA

The third way the love of God will be demonstrated in the church is to meet the needs of the FTA. The greatest demonstration of love is when you are motivated to meet needs. That is what compassion does. God meets our greatest need because He loves us. "God so loved the world that He gave..." (John 3:16). God gave His Son; Jesus gave His Divinity. The Lord is asking you to give your time to invest in a stranger to change them into a disciple of Jesus.

Jesus took the risk of leaving Heaven to be rejected by the world. Jesus left the familiar of Heaven for the natural realm of man. Jesus left the comfort of His Father's presence to meet us at our point of need. This moment with the FTA is our moment to demonstrate the love of God to the FTA, and to demonstrate to the King Jesus that you are truly His disciple. You will take the risk of being rejected; you will leave your comfort zone; you will step out of the familiar to become a leader just like King Jesus.

This is your moment to demonstrate the Kingdom of Heaven. It is your moment to experience your God-moment as you invade the darkness of the victim with the love of God. It is your moment to bring the Kingdom of Heaven to earth.

It is the moment the devil hates. The reason the FTA's mind is filled with excuses not to attend church, and is distracted from attending church for months is because he is doing everything he can to stop that God-moment when Heaven invades his darkness. The reason your mind is filled with fears, self-doubts, unbelief, and pictures of past defeats because he does not want this moment ever to occur—because at that moment you are plundering the strongman's house.

How does a God-moment happen? When you ask a simple question: If God would do a miracle in your life this week, what would you want Him to do for you? Your prayer is the portal through which the Kingdom of Heaven invades their life. Your prayer is what the devil wants never to occur.

When you ask that question you are declaring the purpose of the Kingdom of God: for God to invade their life with His love and power to change their life, to deliver them from the oppression of the devil. That question is pregnant with a declaration that the Kingdom of Heaven is on the earth. You are declaring that the Lord wants to do a miracle in their life. You are giving them the hope they are looking for. You are demonstrating the love they desperately need from God. You are proclaiming that the Kingdom of Heaven has come because you are in their life. You are saying to them, "You are blessed because the Spirit of God is in me, and you are about to encounter the Kingdom and rule of God, because when I pray God's Kingdom comes."

But so many Christians say, "I can't do that." If that is what you are thinking, then you need to be trained, equipped, and empowered so you can demonstrate the Kingdom of Heaven on earth. The beginning of that training will equip you to earn the right to be the change-leader in their life. You need relational skills, interview skills, and communication skills—the skills that invite people to tell you, "This is the miracle I need today. This is where I need God to invade my life today." Then you pray, believing Heaven is invading hell because you pray.

## IDENTIFYING DIVINE APPOINTMENTS BY THE ANNOUNCEMENTS

Often FTAs come to church late and leave early. We cannot provide them with personal care and ministry if we do not know where they are located in the sanctuary.

The Care Ministry goal is 100 percent connection with 100 percent of the FTA, 100 percent of the time! Why? Because we do not know who the divine appointment is and we do not know who the Lord has brought to our church. We will not know unless we minister to every FTA. Not every FTA is a divine appointment; not every FTA is going to become part of your church. But we don't want the FTA that God has led to our church to leave and not know the love of God. We do not want him/her to miss their divine moment at our church. We do not want to miss the divine moment for our life. We do not want to miss God, so we are very proactive.

## NEED-FULFILLMENT WELCOME

The welcome to the FTA is value driven. The welcome to the FTA is given by the senior pastor because what the pastor does defines what is important. The FTA needs to know they are important to the pastor—because when the FTA is important to the pastor, they are important to the church.

Here is an example of a pastoral welcome:

"We want to welcome all First-Time Attenders who are here today. We don't believe it is an accident you are here today, but a divine appointment. You see, we have prayed for you to be here today, and we believe God has brought you here because He wants to do a miracle in our life, and He wants us to help you find your miracle. If you would fill out our prayer request form, our staff will pray for you this week, and we have a team of people who will pray for you every day this week. We want you to know you are not alone with your need any longer; you are not alone with your problem. We are here to help you find God's miracle for your life. I want to meet you personally after church, and we have a wonderful hospitality room especially for you because you are important to us."

## POST-SERVICE MINISTRY

If a victim of darkness has not had an opportunity to receive the ministry of the Spirit from a God-multiplier, it must happen before they leave church. We believe the Lord has led someone to His Church to experience a God-moment that will change their lives forever. There is a miracle in God's House today, and we must find it. We can no long grieve the Spirit of God by ignoring the victims of darkness who are important to Him.

The only way the enemy will not distract us from those God-moments is to have it settled and set solidly in our hearts: In this house, God's appointments will be kept! I don't know about the church down the road, but I do know, in this house, the people God honors us by sending to us will be met with the love, mercy, and Spirit of God so they will discover the Kingdom of Heaven in this place. In this church, Heaven invades darkness. In this church, we destroy the works of the devil! That is what we do here.

That faith makes us very proactive, but not pushy. The Spirit of God is not pushy; the Spirit of God is gentle and will not violate the will of another. He gives them the right to go to hell if they so choose. We invite by our love, we invite with our friendship, we invite with our questions, but we do not push.

## PASTOR WILL MEET EVERY FTA

After the FTA has received ministry by the Care Team member, the team member says, "I know the pastor would really enjoy meeting you. Could I take you to meet him for a brief time?" Then the Care Team member escorts the FTA to wherever the pastor may be, introduces the FTA to the pastor, then waits to make sure they are cared for and says good-bye to them.

I contacted a pastor after implementing the Care Ministry asking him how it impacted the church. His response was, "My church is abuzz." I ask why is your church abuzz? He said last Sunday his church of 300 had 27 FTAs. Of the 250 people in the sanctuary, 50 were attending for a month or less, and his church members were abuzz about all the new people. He told me a story why his church had so many visitors.

An FTA couple attended church and met the pastor in the hospitality room. They told him the reason they were in church for the first time in over 20 years was that their business was going upside down. (They needed God.) After listening to them, the pastor prayed for them and their business. After the prayer the wife looked at the pastor and said, "You are a *good* pastor." That was the God-moment when he became their pastor. A simply prayer of faith, a demonstration of the love of God, and their hearts were bonded to the pastor. The 27 FTAs that Sunday were the result of them and others telling their friends: "If you want to attend a church where you will be loved, come with me this Sunday." That is how unusual it is for people to find a church where the love of God is authentically given to the strangers that attend. That is how this church grew by 16 percent in a month.

## TRACKING SYSTEM

Then we begin the process of evaluating the results of the ministry. We collect the tracking system cards and report to the pastor about each FTA. We are capturing information that will be helpful, providing ministry to go forward. The tracking system card for the next step, the Pursuit Ministry, is then distributed to the team members.

## PURSUIT MINISTRY

What is the Pursuit Ministry? It is the second step in making a disciple. It is pursuing the relationship by continuing to communicate authentic care and love through deposits of love.

### Jesus' Story About the Pursuit Ministry

*What man of you, having an hundred sheep, if he lose one of them, doth not leave the ninety and nine in the wilderness, and go after that which is lost, until he find it? And when he hath found it, he layeth it on his shoulders, rejoicing. And when he cometh home, he calleth together his friends and neighbours, saying unto them, Rejoice with me; for I have found my sheep which was lost* (Luke 15:4-6).

This is the story of the pursuit ministry. The first principle of the pursuit ministry is in regards to the motivation. The motivation is not compassion for the lost sheep that will be destroyed. The first motivation to go after the lost sheep is that it is "my sheep." The biggest disconnect we have is emotionally distancing ourselves from the wounded. We don't feel responsibility because they are not mine; therefore, we do not get involved.

***The lost sheep belong to you. They are given to you by your Father.*** The sheep that walk into your church, the wounded FTA, we are to take ownership of them as if they were part of our small group, and we were close to them. We must have the attitude of being vested in this person, an attitude that says, "You belong to me, so I will leave the comfort of the congregation and I will go on the journey until you will let me pick you up on my shoulders."

The shoulder is a symbol of government. When you pick up a lost and wounded sheep and place them upon your shoulders, that means you are covering them with the spiritual authority you have, which they do not have. You are protecting them with your prayers. You are covering them with your faith. You are carrying them in their walk when they cannot walk.

Sometimes we don't want to get involved with others because we just don't know what problems we are going to encounter. Obviously, you cannot take on the burdens of the world, but you can journey after one lost person—one person wounded by the devil who hates them and wants to destroy them (that is what *lost* means; the destroyer is upon them). So you invest time in carrying them upon your shoulder of prayer, interceding for them, fighting for them; the journey will be one of prayer, and one of care—investing in another so they will be delivered from the destroyer.

This pursuit ministry is the step many people fail to do, and therefore they never really become a God-multiplier. Without the pursuit ministry, the steps from the kingdom of darkness to the Kingdom of Heaven are difficult to complete.

This is the season when it is very important for continued investment into the lives of the new disciple. When you do not see the vision of yourself as a God-multiplier to lead someone on the journey, you will not be motivated to lead them on the breakthrough journey. The victim then falls back into the darkness.

Why we are pursuing relationships to make disciples?

## Example of Old Women Making "Personal Contact"

I once interviewed a pastor who told me their church had "personal follow-up." I asked him what that meant? He proudly told me, "We have two 'old ladies' who like to talk to people on the phone. So I give them the visitor cards and they call the visitors up, tell them we were glad they attended church with us, and invite them back."

I asked this pastor, "Have these two sisters ever met the visitors at church before they contacted them?" He responded, "Well, no." Then I asked him, "What is the difference between a stranger from CMI calling you up at 6:00 pm selling you phone service, and a stranger from a church calling you up to sell you church service? None at all. That is why you must earn the right the first Sunday the FTA attends your church."

# FOLLOW UP

Why does the pursuit ministry require 20 percent of your congregation? In years past, my wife attended a certain church, but she would also travel with me sometimes. The church she attended had a program called "telecare." When she would miss a certain number of Sunday services, the computer would flag her name, and she would receive a call. The person would say, "Hi Cheryl. I calling to tell you that Pastor So-and-So loves you and so do I." Well, that was hard to believe because neither the pastor nor this woman had ever met my wife. This phone call violated the principle of authenticity and relationships.

Finally, after receiving this contact a few times, my wife decided she did need some relationships in the church, so when this woman called my wife to tell her again how much Pastor So-and-So loves you and so do I, my wife said, "You know, I don't know anyone in church. Could I meet you after church this Sunday?" The woman reacted and said, "No, I'm too busy."

Why did that woman tell my wife no? Because she had a list of 50 people to contact that night to tell them she loved them, and she did not have the time nor the desire to be involved in the lives of 50 people!

We must have recruited and trained members ready to develop a relationship with people so they can become part of the Body within the church.

## BIBLICAL PRINCIPLES OF THE PURSUIT MINISTRY TO MAKE A DISCIPLE

First, it is good to see why the maintenance culture is not making disciples, but simply church members. Maintenance-culture churches do not meet needs outside of the building. The maintenance culture attempts to produce commitment out of convenience. The goal in the maintenance culture is to "dummy down" the ministry, dilute it so it does not require any commitment from the person who is giving the ministry, just get someone to be involved with the "visitation program." The result is that the person who receives the ministry does not become a disciple, but just a church member. A church member can only make a church member.

So the enemy wins and everyone in the Kingdom of Heaven loses. The Christian loses the reward and sense of significance by changing someone's life, and the FTA loses because he does not see the authentic Kingdom of Heaven. He only sees the diluted maintenance culture as a counterfeit.

That first Sunday you must "earn the right" for ongoing contact/ministry. The goal of this ministry is to make a disciple. A disciple is a follower of a leader. A leader is able to lead another because they have "earned the right" to lead. The more deposits of love, the more ministry invested into the FTA, the more of the Spirit of God they encounters, the more they will want to follow. Earning the right is what God-multipliers do. They invest in people to lead them into the Kingdom of Heaven. When you invest in someone, you become more valuable to them because you see value in them, and you make them more valuable. *That* is loving your neighbor as yourself.

## LEADERSHIP MINISTRY

For years I used the common church growth term "assimilation." Assimilation is what an institution does. Leading someone into the Kingdom is what an individual does. Becoming a part of the Body is the result of being bonded to members of the Body by love. Someone in the Body must lead the person outside of the Body into the Body. That is effective assimilation. Church membership classes do not make anyone a part of the Body, neither do tasks. It is love that does that. The Leadership ministry is the third step in making a disciple. It is *bonding* the wounded to the Body of Christ by leading them in their journey to become part of the Body of Christ.

> *But the father said to his servants, Bring forth the best robe, and put it on him; and put a ring on his hand, and shoes on his feet: And bring hither the fatted calf, and kill it; and let us eat, and be merry: For this my son was dead, and is alive again; he was lost, and is found. And they began to be merry (Luke 15:22-24).*

Leadership ministry is a heart attitude of rejoicing and celebration for the one who was lost to be part of the family. The reason the lost are not important to the church is because we cannot kill the fatted calf; we cannot throw a party; we cannot make the lost feel special because we might offend the elder brother. So, to make everyone equal, the finding of the lost is signified by a candle lit or an announcement made.

The reason the church is so ineffective in making disciples is that we are bound by fear of offending those who do not care if the lost are found. They do not care if the wounded are healed. So the church remains silent when all of Heaven is rejoicing.

The maintenance culture will never rejoice at the lost being found. It will never want to invest the time nor the money in killing the fatted calf. The maintenance-culture attitude toward rescuing the lost is "That is what we must do but it really isn't important enough to get excited about it."

The Leadership ministry begins with the heart of the Father that is looking for the lost son, sees him "afar off," runs to him, restores all of his blessings to him, makes him feel like he is part of the family immediately. There is not a process to enter into the family; he is family, and we are restoring to him the blessings of the family of God. It is an attitude that the wounded-saved is just as important as the people who have been in church the longest. It is an attitude that originates from the heart of the Father that says, "As a shepherd seeks out his flock, so I will seek out My scattered sheep (see Ezek. 34:12)." It is the vision of God that is bigger than the church building. It is the capacity to see your church bigger than the people who attend and understand the scattered sheep are part of your church. They are worth as much as the Sunday school teacher, as much as the elder who has been on the board for 20 years. We must have the eyes and heart of God to respond like Heaven.

There is a stark contrast between Heaven and the maintenance culture. The Kingdom of Heaven is what the church is to bring to earth. But while Heaven is rejoicing, the church is silent. While all the myriads and myriads of angels rejoice over the name of one person who is delivered from the destroyer, the church lights a candle because what is important to the maintenance culture is not important to Heaven, what is important to Heaven is not important to the maintenance culture.

## RESULT OF LEADING INTO THE BODY

*From whom the whole body, joined and knit together by what every joint supplies, according to the effective working by which every part does its share, causes growth of the body for the edifying of itself in love* (Ephesians 4:16).

This is what the purpose is of being part of the Body of Christ. The joints of relationships fits, holds, and supplies, so that every part (person) does its share, causing the growth (both spiritual and numerical) for the strengthening of itself in love. The maintenance-culture objective is not fitting and holding to function, but only to get people to attend. The maintenance culture sabotages the work of the Spirit because it only sees the church as an institution and operates it as an institution, not a spiritual body.

The structured process is not about the need for tasks to be done, but for relationships to be built. When people have relationships with core workers, they will become core workers. When they have no relationships, they have no one to imitate and they follow the path of least resistance back into the comfort zone they were in before, but now the only difference is that their comfort zone includes a meeting on Sunday. If they are not relationally connected to anyone, they will not remain in the fellowship. They need four friends in one month, or they feel disconnected and leave.

The goal is an IID: a person Initiated into the Kingdom of Heaven, Integrated into the Body, and a Disciple relating with another disciple who will show them how to live in this new culture, vision, and mission for life.

## PRINCIPLES OF LEADERSHIP

- **Love bonds people to church**—relational bonding, not tasks. You don't "plug people in." People are not electrical appliances plugged into a task meeting the needs of the church. You cannot love what you do not value. The reason the FTA is not bonded by love into the church is because we do not value them. We do not invest in them because we do not love them.

- **Nurturing groups are ineffective in bonding FTAs into the Body.**

Typically, when any type of small group has met for 12 months or more, they become relationally closed. They will allow visitors to attend their group meetings if that is what the church policy is, but their heart attitude is a closed one. It is not because the people in the group are mean. It is because they have all the relationships and friends they need.

When a FTA attends a small group, and everyone has already developed their relationships within the group, the FTA encounters a relational wall. The wall is there because everyone in the group has friends and the FTA is not needed by anyone in the group. The FTA hits the wall. It is a kind wall; it is Christian wall; but it is a wall that says I don't need you to be my friend because I have all the friends I need.

A pastor told me the following story. A music teacher started attending his church in the fall, having recently moved into town. He asked her to lead the choir in the Christmas cantata. She practiced with the choir for several months and they had a wonderful performance because of this woman's expertise. The pastor told me, "I thought for sure I had her 'plugged in' to a high profile ministry, but," he continued, "when the Christmas performance was over she left the church." He was shocked. She was plugged in. He called her to ask why she decided to leave the church. Her response was, "I don't know anyone in the church."

How could that be? She practiced weekly with the choir. Everyone knew her. But the choir was a "closed group." They all already had their friends, and they did not need another friend. The choir's attitude was, "You can make us a better choir, but I am not going to be your friend, because I have all the friends I need."

Nurturing groups are ineffective in leading FTAs into the church. You must have structures where the people understand and accept the vision and goal of making disciples for Jesus. When the vision and purpose of the group is for nurture, fellowship, and evangelism, only the first two objectives will ever be fulfilled. Ministry to the wounded must be the vision of the group, and the nurture and fellowship are for the purpose of supporting the vision of ministry.

• Relationships are the only resource the church has to communicate the love of God. Here is the reason the church does not lead strangers into the core: because church members do not see value in building relationship with the wounded, the FTA. Church members seldom love strangers so they are seldom bonded to the church. Thousands of people are kidnapped by the enemy from the Kingdom of Heaven right out of the church because of the maintenance culture.

# 12

# YOUR FATHER WANTS YOU IN HIS BUSINESS!

When you were born again, you became part of the family of God. You now are part of a heavenly family, and this family has this huge business—the Father's business. It is part of your inheritance. You have a heritage and inheritance from your heavenly Father. He saved you to engage in the Family business. It is a huge business, it is global business, and your Father has chosen you to expand the Family business.

Jesus came to engage in the Family business:

*And He said unto them, How is it that ye sought Me? Wist ye not that I must be about My Father's business?* (Luke 2:49)

What is the Father's business?

*Jesus saith unto them, My meat is to do the will of Him that sent Me, and to finish His work* [business]. *Say not ye, There are yet four months, and then cometh harvest? behold, I say unto you, Lift up your eyes, and look on the fields; for they are white already to harvest* (John 4:34-35).

"*My meat* is to do the will of Him who sent Me and to finish His business." Jesus identified what energized Him, what was the meat or substance of His life. What energized Jesus was the vision and mission of life: to finish His Father's business.

What was the vision and mission of the Father's business that gave Jesus the passion for life? Jesus describes the Father's business—*the harvest.* "Do you not say, yet four months, then comes the harvest? Behold, I say unto you, lift up your eyes, and look unto the fields they are already white unto *harvest.*"

The Harvest is the Father's business, the Family's business. What is the Heavenly Family's business? It is the redemption, the "buying back," of men and women oppressed by the adversary. Our business is to buy back those who have become lost. They do not know the vision for their life. They do not know the mission for their life. They have been deceived to think life is to buy things instead of buy back hurting, wounded, and confused people. They invest their time and life in things and not in people.

The Father's business is loving people. The Family business is investing in people to buy them back for the Father. We are finishing the business just like Jesus because we are buying them back by investing our love, time, energy to become part of the Family.

The Family business is called the harvest because it is an agricultural-type business. We must sow and not sell; we must reap and not close. We must see the signs for sowing, cultivating, and harvest. The Kingdom business is not based upon consumerism of the kingdom of darkness, but upon hearts changed by sowing seeds of love and forgiveness. The Kingdom business is not based upon consumption, but upon giving away what you have.

The Father's business is based upon authentic love communicated by authentic disciples of Jesus demonstrating the heart of God so they will become part of the Family of God.

The Father's business is worth dying for. First, dying to your self. Then dying so others might live. The payback of the Father's business is not in things, but in a life full of value and a life full of significance because you change people. You change them from the kingdom of darkness to the Kingdom of the Son; change them from dark to light; change them from oppressed to free; you change their eternal destiny. You change people.

When a person's life is changed by the love and power of God, there is no paycheck that can match the fulfillment of dark eyes becoming bright, bound souls becoming free, wounded hearts becoming healed.

When you bring the Kingdom of Heaven to earth, the value is greater than a paycheck. It is greater than a bonus; it is greater than the car that will define who you are or the house that will express your success.

The Kingdom business is not defined by things, but by people who have been changed by you. You transform people from temporal life ending in hell to eternal life with the Father. You change the eternal destiny of people and they will be eternally grateful to you that you became part of the Father's business.

The harvest is what energized Jesus because it was His mission of life. The harvest was His vision of life. The harvest is the Father's business. The most fundamental way to be like Jesus is to have His vision of life, and His mission of life—the Father's business.

The Father's business requires an investment to become part of the Family business. It cost Jesus everything to finish the Father's business. His mission and vision of life cost Him everything. So many Christians today are not disciples of Jesus—they are not following Jesus because they are not following the vision and mission that energized Jesus. They are not passionate about the Father's business, the mission. They only have energy to maintain, not fulfill their life and mission.

There are many fine folk who are involved in church business that has nothing to do with the Father's business. They get their reward by being with church folk doing church things, but the Father's business, the Harvest, is never done. They love, but they love each other. They sow, but they sow into each other. They serve, but they serve each other. That is the maintenance culture: church business, but not the Father's business.

The Father's business is the harvest. Jesus' business was the harvest. What energized Him was the harvest. Jesus was passionate about the Harvest Ministry.

How do we get engaged in the Father's business? Jesus said: Lift up your eyes and look. You must have eyes to see the Father's business.

Often church members ignorantly declare, "I don't have a harvest field; everyone I know is already 'saved.'" Or even worse they make declarations of unbelief: "I am in a hard field. Everyone I work with is closed to the gospel, and are sinners. That is why I eat lunch by myself. I just can't stand to be around those sinners."

If you think your life or your church is in a "hard field," closed to the good news, it is only because you are deceived in the maintenance culture. Jesus said, "The fields are already white unto harvest." Whether you see it or not does not change the fact of what Jesus said, "The harvest is already white." Your harvest field is already white. It is already ripe.

Since the Word is true, our harvest is ripe, then why do church members perceive they have no harvest?

*For this people's heart is waxed gross, and their ears are dull of hearing, and their eyes they have closed; lest at any time they should see with their eyes, and hear with their ears, and should understand with their heart, and should be converted, and I should heal them* (Matthew 13:15).

It is the spiritual condition of church members in the prison of the maintenance culture. Their heart is as hard as the unprofitable servant, and they are blinded by the darkness of maintaining their own life.

The problem isn't the harvest field; it's our sight. We have not lifted up our eyes, and we are not looking; that is why we do not see the harvest. There are receptive people, but because we have such a myopic vision we cannot see what the Lord has presented to us. We walk by divine appointments every day because we are not lifting up our eyes, and we are not looking at the fields.

## ANGELS ARE ABOUT THE FATHER'S BUSINESS

The word Jesus uses for "white" is not the natural color of ripened grain. This word is used for the radiant white of heavenly spiritual beings. It is used to describe the white robes, the white stone, and the white, brilliant light of the presence of angels. I want to suggest to you that the reason the harvest is already ripe is because the Father has sent His *angels into the harvest to prepare the hearts of the people for you and me to share the good news.*

Why would angels be involved in the harvest? Why would angels be the brilliant bright light covering the harvest? Because angels have the same mission as Jesus:

*And He shall send His angels with a great sound of a trumpet, and they shall gather together His elect from the four winds, from one end of heaven to the other* (Matthew 24:31).

The angels will gather the harvest at the end of time from the four winds. I suggest that the angels are not waiting for the end of the age to engage in the Father's business. They are right now engaged in the harvest. They are the bright light that Jesus saw on the harvest.

In fact, we are to employ angels in the Father's business. "Are they not all ministering spirits, sent forth to minister for them who shall be heirs of salvation?" (Heb. 1:14)

Our inheritance in the Father's business is received when we engage angels in the harvest. They are sent forth so our inheritance in the Family business can be fulfilled. When we do not engage angels, we will not have has great an inheritance because we need them ministering in the harvest. We must see our harvest field "brilliantly white" unto harvest.

*Fear not: for I am with thee: I will bring thy seed from the east, and gather thee from the west; I will say to the north, Give up; and to the south, Keep not back: bring My sons from far, and My daughters from the ends of the earth; even every one that is called by My name: for I have created him for My glory, I have formed him; yea, I have made him* (Isaiah 43:5-7).

Angels are commissioned to go to the four winds to gather the elect. Angels are preparing the hearts of lost, confused, disoriented, and deceived people to receive the good news about Jesus Christ. They have a very limited ministry—angels can only prepare; disciples must proclaim.

Angels are in the harvest, preparing the hearts of the lost. They wait for a disciple to be about the Father's business. Angels cannot fulfill their mission without disciples sharing the good news. The Father's business cannot be done only by what Jesus did on the cross. The Father's business cannot be done only by the convicting work of the Holy Spirit. The Father's business cannot be done by the ministry of angels.

The work Jesus finished will only be fulfilled when His disciples are employed in the Father's business. Jesus' work cannot fulfill it; the work of the Holy Spirit cannot fulfill it; angels cannot fulfill it. If those who are redeemed are not about the Father's business, we will frustrate the heavenly mission of Jesus, the Holy Spirit, and angels.

*Likewise, I say unto you, there is joy in the presence of the angels of God over one sinner that repenteth* (Luke 15:10).

Why do the angels of God rejoice when one sinner repents? Because they are about the Father's business. They have the mission to be in the harvest preparing the hearts of the lost to discover the love and salvation in the Kingdom of Heaven.

When a disciple shares the gospel to lead someone to the Lord, the Bible says all the angels in Heaven rejoice when a sinner repents. Why do angels rejoice? Because they are in the Father's business. You will become known among the angels when the Father's business becomes your business.

*And when He is come, He will reprove the world of sin, and of righteousness, and of judgment* (John 16:8).

Finally, the Holy Spirit is in the Father's business. His ministry is to convict the world of the sin of unbelief, the righteousness that Jesus reigns over the Kingdom of Heaven, and of the judgment of the prince of this world.

How important is the Harvest? Jesus tells us the Harvest is the Father's business, and He is about His Father's business. The angels are in the Father's business; the Holy Spirit is in the Father's business. Those who are redeemed, bought back from the kingdom of darkness, are in the Father's business. The Father's business is the harvest.

*The harvest is the Father's business.*

*The Father's business is Jesus' business.*

*The Father's business is the Holy Spirit's business.*

*The Father's business is the angels' business.*

*The Father's business is the Church's business.*

*The Father's business is your business.*

Everything and everyone related to the Father is engaged in the Father's business.

The Father's business is buying back the lost souls who do not have a vision or mission of life. They are deceived on a journey that is destroying and will destroy their lives. We are in the business of buying them back—redeeming them from the pit.

## THE FATHER'S BUSINESS HAS ETERNAL WAGES

*And he that reapeth receiveth wages, and gathereth fruit unto life eternal: that both he that soweth and he that reapeth may rejoice together. And herein is that saying true, One soweth, and another reapeth. I sent you to reap that whereon ye bestowed no labour: other men laboured, and ye are entered into their labours* (John 4:36-38).

Why should you be in your heavenly Father's business? Because you can't beat the pay. Jesus said, "He that reaps [in the harvest] *receives wages...for eternal life.*" Many Christians' perspective of Heaven is a classless egalitarian existence. When we arrive at the pearly gates, we will be given a harp and assigned a place in the heavenly choir, and we will sing praises to God for eternity.

If that is the only experience in Heaven, then why will the disciples in the Father's business, the Family business, be given wages for eternal life? If some will receive wages, it is because they will be able to invest them or spend them for eternity. If you are not involved in the Father's business, you will not have any wages when you get to Heaven. You'll be eternally broke when you get to Heaven. You will be the unprofitable servant, and for eternity you will have no profit.

The other blessing in the harvest ministry is that you will reap where you have not sown, and you will gather where you have not labored. That is a Kingdom principle and blessing. When you get into the harvest and the blessings of the Kingdom, you will begin to reap and you have not sown, and you will gather and you have not labored! This is when the blessings begin to multiply to you.

Jesus also said in the harvest ministry we would gather "eternal fruit." What is fruit?

*Ye have not chosen Me, but I have chosen you, and ordained you, that ye should go and bring forth fruit, and that your fruit should remain: that whatsoever ye shall ask of the Father in My name, He may give it you* (John 15:16).

When the Father chose you and me before the foundations of the earth, He chose us to bring forth fruit, and that our fruit should remain for eternity. What type of fruit is a disciple to bring forth?

Many correlate the fruit of the Spirit (love, joy, peace, longsuffering, gentleness, goodness, faith, meekness, and temperance, as listed in Galatians 5:22) with the fruit that Jesus wants to see from His disciples.

But in Genesis the Bible defines fruit as "after his kind":

*And God said, Let the earth bring forth grass, the herb yielding seed, and the fruit tree yielding fruit after his kind, whose seed is in itself, upon the earth: and it was so* (Genesis 1:11).

The fruit of the Spirit is after His kind—it is what the Spirit produces. A disciple does not produce the fruit of the Spirit; the Spirit produces the fruit of the Spirit. What type of fruit then does the disciple produce? What is the fruit of a disciple? After his kind. A disciple produces a disciple. The fruit of a disciple is another disciple. The eternal fruit in John 4:35 is the fruit of a disciple. The fruit that Jesus has chosen us to produce is another disciple. The Spirit produces the fruit of the Spirit in a disciple so a disciple can produce the fruit of a disciple in the world.

Jesus said, "This is how My Father is glorified, when you produce a lot of fruit and prove to be My disciples" (see John 15:8 HCSB).

In the maintenance-culture church, members have the proof they are members; they attend church and give money. When people give to the church and attend church, that is the proof they are members of the church. Jesus is not looking for maintenance-culture church members,

He is looking for His disciples. How does Jesus identify His disciples? Those who have the fruit of a disciple. The fruit of a disciple is another disciple.

What is the proof that Jesus is looking for? The fruit of a disciple, not church attendance, offerings, and being a nice person. Those characteristics can be accomplished in a disciplined person without the life of God. (Buddhist monks are nice; they attend meetings and give, but that does not prove they are disciples of Jesus.)

The proof Jesus is looking for is the spiritual dynamic of the Life of God in you to produce another life. The spiritual dynamic of the maintenance-culture church member produces attendance and giving. The spiritual dynamic of a disciple produces another disciple.

There will be a moment when you must prove you are a disciple of Jesus Christ. Did you follow Him in giving all for the Father's business?

*For we must all appear before the judgment seat of Christ, so that each one may receive what is due for what he has done in the body, whether good or evil* (2 Corinthians 5:10 ESV).

The destination to the journey of life for those who name the name of Jesus is the judgment seat of Christ. That destination will determine your eternal destiny. In that defining moment when you approach the Judgment Seat of Christ, you do not want to come alone.

Here is the possible conversation between the barren, unprofitable, maintenance-culture church member who ignored the Father's business for their business:

**Jesus:** "Why are you here by yourself? Where is the proof you are my disciple?

**Fearful maintenance-culture church member:** "I made it. That's the proof. I don't smoke. I don't cuss. I don't chew. That is the proof I am your disciple."

**Jesus:** No, why are you here in front of me by yourself? Where is the proof you are my disciple?

**Fearful maintenance culture church member:** Well, I went to church every Sunday."

**Jesus:** "Then why are you here by yourself? Prove to Me you are My disciple."

**Fearful maintenance-culture church member:** "I went to Sunday school class. See my perfect attendance certificate? I never missed Sunday school class."

**Jesus:** "Then why are you here by yourself? Prove to Me that you are My disciple."

**Fearful maintenance-culture church member:** "Jesus, I read my Bible every day."

**Jesus:** "Then why are you here by yourself? Prove to Me that you are My disciple."

**Fearful maintenance-culture church member:** "I prayed almost every day."

**Jesus:** "Then why are you here by yourself? Prove to Me you are My disciple."

**Fearful maintenance-culture church member:** "Jesus, I did what they told me to do. I attended church and Sunday school class; I read my Bible; I was a good Christian."

**Jesus:** "Then why are you here by yourself? Prove to Me you are My disciple."

**Fearful maintenance-culture church member:** "Jesus, what do You want from me?"

**Jesus:** "Where's the proof? Prove to me you are My disciple.

You see, the maintenance-culture church member thinks the proof of being a good church member, church attendance, being nice—the maintenance culture values is the proof King Jesus is looking for. Jesus doesn't care if you are a member of a church, the Kiwanis club, or the country club. He wants proof that you are His disciple. The proof that you are a disciple of Jesus Christ is another disciple.

The moment you will need to prove you are a disciple is when you stand before the Lamb of God who sacrificed all for the Father's business. I don't want to stand before Jesus alone. I want to approach the

Judgment Seat with lots of other disciples with me, disciples I have made. I want to be able to say to Jesus, "Let me introduce to You the disciples I have made, and the fruit that I produced. I have the proof the life of God was transformed me because that life in me transformed victims into victors.

Darrell Massier was the first person I recruited in the Care Ministry. In the first six years of the Care Ministry, Darrell led 500 people to the Lord. Five hundred people to whom angels were ministering to receive Jesus. Every time Darrell made himself available to the Lord and partnered with angels for the mission Jesus died for to make disciples of 500 people, the angels rejoiced not only over the sinner that repented, but Darrell who worked with them in the Father's business.

Five hundred times Darrell's name has resounded throughout Heaven as angels rejoiced over Darrell for working with them in the Father's business. Five hundred times Darrell made Heaven happy.

When Darrell approaches the judgment seat of Christ, he will have hundreds of people with him to introduce to Jesus. When it is his turn to approach the judgment seat, and his name is called out, all of the angels in Heaven will turn to see Darrell. Angels will rush over to meet him and will applaud as he approaches the judgment seat. He will approach the judgment seat with thanksgiving, joy, and rejoicing because he was about the Father's business.

You have a choice how you will invest your time. You can be employed in the Father's business, rejoicing with the angels, or you can be employed by a man, and spend eternity regretting that you were not like King Jesus, energized by the Father's business.

You can be known by the president of your company, or you can be known by the angels in Heaven. You can make your boss happy, or you can make Heaven happy. How you invest your time here is how you will enjoy eternity there. If you are sitting here, you will be sitting there. If you are a God-multiplier on earth, you will be rich and famous in the Kingdom of Heaven.

# Author Information

Ken's ministry is in thousands of churches across the U.S. and 16 foreign countries. There are several conferences and resources available for you and your church:

## Conferences:

### Breakthrough Conference

This is a weekend conference with the purpose is to recruit and train 20 percent of your congregation to transform visitors into disciples in your local church.

### Maximize Your Church

One of the greatest needs in the church is to change the culture. Culture change is not accomplished through an institutional application, but through individual transformation. This leadership conference shows you how to transform the church culture to a Kingdom-culture.

### Maximize Your Life

This conference focuses on the life skills and ministry skills necessary to live a high capacity and high performance life. This conference will change your life.

# Resources:

### Maximize Your World

This is a study guide for you to see the victims of darkness in your kingdom-realm. It will prepare you to invade the kingdom of darkness and plunder victims out of darkness to become victors in the Kingdom of Heaven.

# Contact Information:

You can contact Ken Houts, founder and executive director of Care Ministries International and Maximize Ministries, at www.careministries.net or 1-800-769-4769.

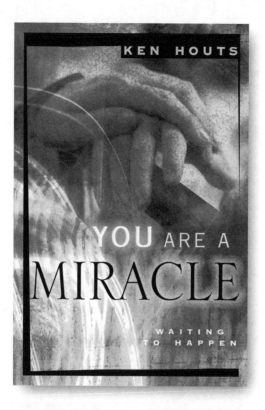

## YOU ARE A MIRACLE—WAITING TO HAPPEN

*You Are a Miracle* is jam-packed with practical aids and insights on how you can become a miracle in the lives of other people. Rather than waiting around for your own miracle to happen, you will discover the *real joy* of Christian living—making miracles happen in the lives of others!

*In this book you'll learn:*
- Three miracle-working questions that release the power of God.
- Seven signs of a miracle waiting to happen.
- Three skills of love that empower you to impact people with Jesus.
- Five levels of communication.
- Seven ways people experience pain and how to meet their needs.
- Skills for making lifelong friends.
- Plus much more!

There are miracles all around you waiting to happen—broken lives desperate for your love and support. *You Are a Miracle* will give you the vision to see those miracles and the spiritual tools to make someone's miracle become a reality.

**ISBN 0-7684-2308-2**

### Available at your local Christian bookstore.

Additional copies of this book and other
book titles from DESTINY IMAGE are
available at your local bookstore.

Call toll-free: 1-800-722-6774.

Send a request for a catalog to:

**Destiny Image® Publishers, Inc.**
P.O. Box 310
Shippensburg, PA 17257-0310

*"Speaking to the Purposes of God for This
Generation and for the Generations to Come"*

**For a complete list of our titles,
visit us at www.destinyimage.com**